Language, the Learner and the School

Language, the Learner and the School

FOURTH EDITION

Douglas Barnes, James Britton and
Mike Torbe

BOYNTON/COOK PUBLISHERS
HEINEMANN
Portsmouth, NH

BOYNTON / COOK PUBLISHERS
A Division of
HEINEMANN EDUCATIONAL BOOKS, INC.
70 Court Street, Portsmouth, NH   03801
Offices and agents throughout the world

©1990 by Heinemann Educational Books, Inc. Previous editions ©1986 by Douglas Barnes, James Britton, and Mike Torbe; ©1969 and 1971 by Douglas Barnes, James Britton, Harold Rosen, and the London Association for the Teaching of English.

First published 1969, Penguin Books, London
Reprinted 1969
Second edition 1971
Reprinted 1971, 1972, 1973, 1974, 1975, 1976, 1978, 1981
Third edition 1986
Fourth edition published 1990, Boynton / Cook–Heinemann, Portsmouth, NH

Library of Congress Cataloging-in-Publication Data
Barnes, Douglas R.
     Language, the learner and the school / Douglas Barnes, James
Britton, and Mike Torbe. —4th ed.
        p. cm.
        Includes bibliographical references.
        ISBN 0-86709-251-3
        1. Language arts (Secondary) 2. Oral communication.   I. Britton,
James N.   II. Torbe, Mike.   III. Title.
LB1631.B29 1990
373. 13—dc20   89-22228
                                                                                              CIP

Front cover design by Max-Karl Winkler.

Printed in the United States of America
10 9 8 7 6 5 4 3 2 1

Contents

Preface to the Fourth Edition

Wherever you look in the world, those in education are always under pressure because internationally there is such heavy financial and social investment in schools and schooling. There is pressure from outside the system – from politicians, newspapers and television, and parents, who all look for evidence that schools are producing young people with expected kinds of knowledge and skills. There is pressure from those within the system – from administrators, budget controllers, evaluators, and testers – all looking for effectiveness and value for money. And all the time, teachers put professional pressure on themselves as they search for ways of making sure that young people learn effectively.

Whatever the political condition of a society and whatever are currently being looked for as the best outcomes of education, the central encounter is between teachers and young people in school classrooms. It is in the reality of these classrooms and this encounter that all the theories and practices of education come together and are tested as teachers and students talk, listen, read, and write. Young people's talking and writing have a central part in their learning. *Language, the Learner and the School* explores, illustrates, and develops that principle. It is the teacher who plans new experiences, understandings, and activities, but it is the students who must make sense of them. They do this mostly through the talking and writing they do, activities that enable them to relate new ideas and experiences to their existing understanding of the world. The three papers that make up this book explore how language can be a means of learning; how teachers' classroom strategies influence this; and how both together make effective learning more likely.

Our first concern in the book is to show that classroom talk, when properly managed, can make a significant contribution to learning. We say 'properly managed' because it is not always easy to put such opportunities into practice in the crowded and complex life of the classroom. We are pleased, therefore, that *Language, the Learner and the School* in its previous editions persuaded many teachers to take a critical look at their teaching: it encouraged them to consider afresh how they talked to their students, and to ask themselves whether their lessons gave learners enough opportunity to 'think aloud' in speech and in writing.

The line of thought explored in these three papers originated in the discussion of a group of teachers and academics in London, who carried out informal studies in their own classrooms. James Britton's paper incorporates some of the material they collected, and it develops ideas about how discussing in small groups helps young people to examine and reconstruct their understanding of the world. During the early 1970s, interest in the kind of ideas presented here quickly spread to teachers of subjects other than English, and the expression 'language across the curriculum' came to be used and is now widespread throughout the English-speaking world.

Douglas Barnes's paper describes an investigation into how the language used by teachers and pupils during lessons is likely to influence the learning that takes place. He goes on to discuss more recent developments along this line of thought. Mike Torbe looks at language in the school as a whole: he examines what can be learnt from attempts to establish language policies in schools, and discusses the implications of linguistic and ethnic diversity for learning.

Teaching is a highly skilled activity that requires from the teacher an immediate response to events as they develop. He or she must attend not only to long-term goals but also to the urgent details of the student's participation in the lesson. The teacher must judge instantly whether the moment requires a suggestion, an invitation to explain, a discouraging glance, an anecdote, a joke, a reprimand, or the setting of a new task. These immediate decisions depend necessarily upon intuitive judgement, but these intuitions themselves can be reflected upon, sharpened, and related more precisely to long-term goals and values. What is likely to help teachers towards a more principled and effective intuition? We believe that the best way is to refine what teachers already possess – a sensitivity to the ebb and flow of meaning in conversation – and then to apply it to the day-to-day life of the classroom.

Douglas Barnes   James Britton   Mike Torbe

Part One
Language in
the Secondary Classroom

Douglas Barnes

This is an account of a study of teaching which was carried out with two groups of teachers. The original study took place in 1966–7 and was published in 1969; part of the text thus derives from the sixties. However, revising the account fifteen years later has provided an opportunity for me to add a reflexive commentary from a changed point of view. Some of the changes have been made solely in the interest of clarity. Whenever a new passage expresses a radical change of view, however, I have made explicit that it is written from the later perspective.

In October 1966, newly appointed to the University of Leeds Institute of Education (now the School of Education), I undertook to lecture on 'Language and Education' to teachers seconded for advanced diploma courses, and concurrently to teach a series of seminars on the same topic to a smaller group of those teachers. It was at that point that I recollected a conversation with Harold Rosen in which he had suggested that it would be very interesting to follow a class through a day's schooling, recording all of the written and spoken language activities in which they were either receivers or producers. The original collection of materials thus made no pretension to 'research': teachers who were members of the 1966 and 1967 groups tape-recorded lessons as a basis for discussion in the seminars, in the hope of understanding better the part played by language in classroom learning and thereby improving their teaching. Each teacher transcribed one or two lessons, analysed them according to a scheme which I provided, and then presented the results in a seminar. This paper in its original form arose from the topics and ideas accumulated through the two years of seminars.

When the study began I saw it as a study of language, and particularly of the way in which linguistic forms and styles seemed at times to create a barrier between teacher and taught. However, as the analytical scheme will show, I was also interested in the processes of communication by which teachers offered to their pupils some part in the formulation of what counted as knowledge. From my present perspective, these latter processes seem of greater importance.

Obtaining Material

Our purpose was to record the whole language environment of the children during lesson-time. We were interested in both spoken and written language, and in the child as producer and receiver. We expected our sources to include:

Spoken language

(a) The teacher's oral exposition.
(b) The teacher's questions, and the resulting teacher-initiated exchanges.
(c) Discussion – i.e. partly pupil-initiated.
(d) Language used in the course of the teacher–pupil relationship – e.g. persuasion, criticism, relationship-establishing.
(e) Pupil to pupil language.

Written language

(a) Textbooks used during the lesson.
(b) Teachers' notes – duplicated, dictated, or copied from the blackboard.
(c) Writing – teacher-defined (i) in form.
                                    (ii) in content.
(d) Writing – wholly or partly pupil-defined.
(e) Other written material – e.g. charts.

The investigators obtained permission to go into lessons with a tape-recorder, recorded the lessons, and supplemented the recording with notes of:

(a) The children's contributions, which were often incomprehensible on tape.

(b) Significant actions and gestures accompanying speech.

(c) Writing and diagrams from the blackboard.

(d) Sketches of any apparatus in use.

They also borrowed textbooks and selected exercise books in order to make photocopies of relevant passages.

In 1966 the teachers collaborating with me made separate arrangements to record lessons being taught by teachers whom they knew well. In 1967 I arranged with the headmaster of a comprehensive school to follow a first-year class through a whole day of lessons. (The implications of this are discussed later.) On both occasions the pupils were in about the sixth week of attendance at that secondary school, with the exception of two mathematics lessons in 1966. In 1967 there were two investigators present in each lesson: in both years the tape-recording was transcribed by an investigator who had been present during the lesson (with the exception of Lesson G). The lessons can be tabulated:

1966

	Secondary modern (mixed)	Comprehensive (mixed)	Grammar (boys)	Grammar (girls)
Maths (2 lessons) Science (3 lessons)	Lesson B (man)	Lesson G (physics) (man) Lesson E (biology) (woman)	Lesson A★ (man) Lesson F (chemistry) (man)	

★ The investigator recorded a second-year class in error.

1966

	Secondary modern (mixed)	Comprehensive (mixed)	Grammar (boys)	Grammar (girls)
Geography/ history (2 lessons)				Lesson C (history) (woman) Lesson D (geography) (woman)
Total	1	2	2	2

Seven lessons were recorded and transcribed, though one was with an older class.

1967

The class chosen was the fourth out of seven first-year streamed classes in a mixed comprehensive school in an industrial area.

During the day seven lessons were recorded, but two (French and drama) have not been transcribed or analysed. The five that remain – which constitute the main body of material – are:

Lesson J   Mathematics (woman)
Lesson K   History (man)
Lesson L   Physics (woman)
Lesson M   English (man)
Lesson N   Religious Education (man)

The Analysis of the Material

The collection and analysis of the classroom material was guided by the following scheme, which directed the investigators' attention:

Douglas Barnes

(*a*) *Teacher's questions*

Analyse *all* questions asked by the teacher into these categories:

1. *Factual* ('What?' questions)
   (i) naming
   (ii) information
2. *Reasoning* ('How?' and 'Why?' questions)
   (i) 'closed' reasoning – recalled sequences
   (ii) 'closed' reasoning – not recalled
   (iii) 'open' reasoning
   (iv) observation
3. *'Open' questions not calling for reasoning*
4. *Social*
   (i) control ('Won't you ... ?' questions)
   (ii) appeal ('Aren't we ... ?' questions)
   (iii) other

Notes on questions

Naming questions ask pupils to give a name to some phenomenon without requiring them to show insight into its use.

Reasoning questions require pupils to 'think aloud' – to construct, or reconstruct from memory, a logically organized sequence.

Recall questions are concerned with summoning up required knowledge from memory.

Closed questions have only one acceptable answer; whereas to

Open questions a number of different answers would be acceptable. Open questions might be factual in some circumstances: for example, a request for 'any fraction', where the range of choices open to the pupil is unusually wide. (It is necessary to check apparently open questions by examining the teacher's reception of pupils' replies, which may show that he will accept only one reply to a question framed in apparently open terms. Such questions might be called 'pseudo-questions'.)

Observation questions are intended to include those questions (about phenomena immediately present to the children) which require them to interpret what they perceive. (There may be difficulty in distinguishing some of these from 'naming questions'.)

Control questions are directed towards imposing the teacher's wishes upon the class.

Appeal questions, which ask pupils to agree, or share an attitude, or remember an experience, are less directive than control questions: that is, it is possible for children to reject them without necessarily giving offence.

(b) *Pupils' participation*

1. Was all speech initiated by the teacher? Note any exchanges initiated by pupils.
   (i) If these were initiated by questions, were they 'What?', 'How?' or 'Why?' questions? Were they directed towards the material studied or towards performing the given tasks?
   (ii) If they were unsolicited statements or comments, how did the teacher deal with them?
2. Were pupils required to express personal responses
   (i) of perception?
   (ii) of feeling and attitude?
3. How large a part did pupils take in the lesson? Were any silent throughout? How large a proportion took a continuous part in discussion?
4. What did pupils' contributions show of their success in following the lesson?
5. How did the teacher deal with inappropriate contributions?

(c) *The language of instruction*

1. Did the teacher use a linguistic register specific to his subject? Find examples of vocabulary and structures characteristic of the register.

2. Did any pupils attempt to use this register? Was it expected of them?
3. What did the teacher do to mediate between the language and experience of his pupils and the language and concepts of the subject?
4. Did the teacher use forms of language which, though not specific to his subject, might be outside the range of eleven-year-olds? Find examples, if any.

(*d*) *Social relationships*

1. How did the relationship between teacher and pupils show itself in language?
2. Were there differences between the language of instruction and the language of relationships? Was the language of relationships intimate or formal? Did it vary during the lesson?

(*e*) *Language and other media*

1. Was language used for any tasks that might have been done better by other means (e.g. pictures, practical tasks, demonstrations)?
2. Were pupils expected to verbalize any non-verbal tasks they engaged in?

Limitations

(a) The sample – even if all twelve lessons are included – is far too small to allow for any statements more positive than hypothesis. Any conclusions must be methodological, or indications for further investigation, or concerned with the appropriateness of such study to the training of teachers, or limited to statements about these lessons and no others.

(b) Most of the teachers in the 1966 sample are mature, confident, and on friendly terms with the one investigator present: there seems no reason to think that the investigation caused any major change in their teaching behaviour. On the other hand, the sample was so diverse as to discourage even the most qualified generalization.

(c) In 1967 the choice of a single class required that the invitation be given to a headmaster, and not to individual teachers. This meant that the teachers whose lessons were investigated were not necessarily very eager to collaborate. In the event, they tended to be young and more disturbed by our presence than were the 1966 teachers. Some were clearly nervous, and even unwilling. Others seemed to have 'over-prepared' the material they were teaching.

(d) Since speakers intuitively adjust their language forms to different audiences, our presence – and that of our tape-recorders – probably caused some non-deliberate changes in language.

(e) The teachers had been told that the investigators were interested in the language used in the lessons. Although they were asked to carry on with normal work, some may have slanted their lesson more towards spoken language than would otherwise have been the case.

Interrelation of Results

As the analytical instrument indicates, the demands made upon the pupils were examined under five heads:

Questions asked by the teacher
The participation demanded of (or allowed to) the pupils
The language used in instruction
The language used in social control
Relationship of language to other activities and media

Clearly these are matters of analytic convenience. The teachers' questions, for example, are drawn from the language of social control and from the language of instruction, having been extracted for more quantitative analysis. The questions about pupil participation require more than description of language: the material is here used to make qualitative judgements about teaching and learning. Something similar is true of the relationship of language to other activities and media. These are not, however, five separate issues; in pursuing them one has the impression of making five different approaches to the same complex of social behaviour. To change one might be to change all.

It will be seen from pp. 15–16 that we sorted teachers' questions into four categories: factual, reasoning, open questions not calling for reasoning, and social. We also distinguished which of the factual and reasoning questions were open-ended and which closed-ended. When we discussed particular questions which occurred in the lessons we had recorded, we did not always find it easy to assign questions to a particular category.

In checking the results for publication I first eliminated all questions which were no more than reformulations of a preceding question that had been unanswered. Then I discovered that in order to arrive at a satisfactory interpretation I had to look at succeeding utterances by teacher or pupils, and sometimes at preceding ones. For example, when a teacher says, 'John, are you working?' this is more likely to be an injunction to continue work than a request for information, as John's reaction to it is likely to show. That is, the functional meaning lay not in the sentence itself but in the way it was being used in that particular interaction. Meaning seemed not to be an adjunct of words alone but to be generated by teachers and pupils from the cultural resources they shared in the classroom. At that time, however, I did not consciously distinguish form from function – I did not meet Austin's[1] idea of 'illocutionary force' until later – and I recorded at that time my uncertainty as to whether the same functional analysis could be reproduced by another analyst. (I realize now that cultural categories of this kind are created in part by the act of categorizing and cannot be handed over unambiguously to another person simply by definition: I was hankering after an objectivity which the very nature of intersubjective meaning probably makes unattainable.)

The table below shows my own analysis of all the questions asked during the five lessons recorded in 1967.

Tables of Teachers' Questions in Five Lessons

Lesson	J Maths	L Science	K History	M English	N R.E
(a) *Analysis of questions*					
Factual (Category 1)	36	9	30	19	21
Reasoning (Category 2)	17	19	4	6	7
Open questions not calling for reasoning (Category 3)	0	0	0	0	0
Social (Category4)	19	5	5	12	9
Total number of questions	72	33	39	37	37
(b) *Open questions*					
Number of open questions (Factual and Reasoning)	9	9	8	12	1
Open questions as % of total	17	32	23·5	48	3·6

Figures of this kind can be taken to represent the teachers' covert interpretation of the nature of what they were teaching – that is, the interpretation *that they were acting upon* whatever they may have told themselves about the purpose of the lesson. And this covert version of their subject is important because it will be 'learnt' by the pupils *as part of the role of being a learner in that subject.*

I am no longer so confident of this as the tone of the above paragraph suggests, for nowadays I would look at the whole of the interaction observed in lessons to determine the roles open to the pupils. There is of course much to be gained from attempting to reduce our overall impression of a lesson to a few indicators that can be quantified, but we must be on our guard because it is possible that a single indicator may be misleading. Nevertheless, the general point still holds that the roles as learners which boys and girls take over in lessons may provide as much important learning as does the content of the curriculum. Since I wrote the above paragraph such oblique social learning has come to be called 'the hidden curriculum'; although the term has been criticized, the idea still seems to me an important one.

What most impressed my students and me in these figures was the predominance of factual over reasoning questions in the three arts subjects lessons, that is, seventy factual questions against seventeen reasoning questions. Typical factual questions were: 'Does anyone know any of the books or poems Homer wrote?' 'Where do you think they kept the lamps?' (The answer had been given in a previous lesson.) 'We call it A A B B A ... and what do we call that?' (The answer finally given by the teacher was 'Rhyming scheme'.) Reasoning questions included: 'Now what makes a language beautiful?' 'Why do you think they used bread for spoons?' 'That second line's not right [refers to metrical pattern]. Why not?' This proportion suggests that the three arts teachers were teaching as though their tasks were more concerned with information than thought. If so, this is the version of the subjects that the children were learning. The teachers would perhaps be surprised to discover this about their teaching and might wish to change it. (Or they might believe that this is a proper proportion between information and thought, in which case it would be difficult to agree with them.) This analysis goes some way towards enabling a teacher to find out about aspects of his teaching of which he may normally be unaware.

Almost equally surprising is the predominance of factual over reasoning questions in the mathematics lesson. This is explained by our decision to categorize as factual questions (a) those which required pupils to count items in a diagram ('How many squares?'), and (b) the kind that, for example, required pupils to know that if a whole is divided into six parts each part is called a sixth (i.e. a naming question, Category 1(i)). The high proportion of reasoning questions in the science lesson well represents the pattern of the lesson: the teacher made several demonstrations to the class and required them to explain to her what was happening, asking for example: 'Why did it go off just at that point?'

Entirely 'open' questions hardly ever occur, so in distinguishing closed from open questions we were in fact distinguishing those cases in which the teacher will accept only a single answer expressed in a relatively predetermined form from those cases in which he will accept either a wide (but not infinite) range of answers, or a small limited range but in any order. Some of the most difficult distinctions arise when the teacher clearly knows the kind of answer he wants, so that the decision to categorize as open or closed rests upon a subjective assessment of the extent to which he wishes his pupils to explore the alternative formulations, relationships and contexts of this reply.

Examples of extremely open questions are: 'Tell me any fraction' and 'What books have you been reading?' When a teacher asked, 'How do we recognize what a limerick is?' he was ready to accept four answers in any order, but it was clear that he knew in advance exactly what these were. Questions of this kind were categorized as 'open', though with some hesitation. Another borderline case was: 'Why did it [a flame] go down?' in answer to which the teacher accepted, 'The gas wasn't coming for it to be burnt', and added, 'There wasn't as much gas spare.' She knew what answer she wanted, but was also willing to accept the pupil's formulation, so – again with hesitation – we categorized this as 'open'.

Although the proportions (given in the table) of open questions to the total number of open and closed questions may not be entirely reliable, their tendency is clear enough. In spite of our perhaps over-generous allocation of doubtful cases to the 'open' category, the proportion is low in all lessons except English. (The open questions in the English lesson were largely ones requiring the pupils to find likenesses between two poems; the teacher accepted a wide range of replies relating either to form or to meaning.) These proportions can be taken to mean that four of the teachers were taking their task to be more a matter of handing over ready-made material, whether facts or processes, than a matter of encouraging pupils to participate actively and to bring their own thoughts and recollections into the conversation. (Very few questions indeed were asked because the teacher was truly ignorant of the answer and wanted to know; the implications of this for the explicitness of replies bear pondering.)

If an analysis such as this were applied to a larger representative sample of first-year lessons and gave similar results to those tabulated above, it would be reasonable for those responsible for curricular planning to ask themselves (i) whether arts subjects *should* at this level be predominantly factual, and (ii) whether more active participation in arts and sciences *might be more effective*. This might lead to questioning whether they wished to encourage pupils in habits of acceptance or habits of improvisation.

Both the 1966 and 1967 lessons provided many examples of what the investigators came to call 'pseudo-questions', since they appeared open but were treated by the teacher as closed. For example, in Lesson L (the 1967 science lesson) the teacher asked:

T   What can you tell me about a bunsen burner, Alan?
P.1 A luminous and non-luminous flame.
T   A luminous and non-luminous flame ... When do you have a luminous flame?
P.1 When there's ... there's oxygen.
T   When the airhole is closed ... When is it a non-luminous flame, Gary?
P.2 When ... when the air-hole is open.
T   Right ... good ...

The original question requires the pupil to abstract from all possible statements about the bunsen burner that one which the teacher's unstated criterion finds acceptable. He is presumably helped to do this by memories of a former lesson on the topic. Our samples suggest that it is not unusual for teachers to ask children to conform to an unstated criterion; children might participate better if the criteria were explicit.

Another group of 'pseudo-questions' appears to relate to classroom procedure but should perhaps be reckoned as 'social' in function. For example, in Lesson F (1966; grammar school; chemistry lesson) has several such questions:

T   Now what we want is a method whereby we can take off this . . . um . . . green material . . . this green stuff off the grass and perhaps one or two of you can suggest how we might do this . . . Yes?

P.1   Boil it.

T   Boil it? What with?

P.1   Some water in a beaker and . . .

T   Yes, there's that method . . . we could do it and . . . um . . . I think probably you could guess how we might be able to do it by what we've already got out in the laboratory. How do you think we might do it?
     [pestle and mortar are on bench]

P.2   Could pound it . . .

T   Pound it up with water . . . and that's exactly what we're going to do.

The teacher having, perhaps necessarily, predetermined the method to be used, asks the question in order to involve his pupils more personally into the activity. But this forces him (a) to interrupt a pupil who is thinking aloud ('some water in a beaker and . . .') and (b) to reject that pupil's reasonable suggestion. It could be argued that both of these are to be avoided for pedagogical reasons.

This passage deserves further comment because it enshrines a fine example of the 'irrelevant prompt'. Initially the teacher asked the question so as to draw the pupils into thinking out the practical problems for themselves. The one suggestion he receives is rejected without explanation of why it is not acceptable, but instead of acknowledging that he is going to have to tell the class the method to be used he directs their attention to the equipment on the bench. This must short-circuit the problem-solving task by presenting the class with the solution in oblique form. Such irrelevant prompts − irrelevant, that is, to the rational analysis of the problem − are quite common in some teaching styles, and seem to provide the teacher − rather than the pupils − with a sense of closure, though it is a meretricious one.

In the 1967 lessons there was not one example of an 'open question not calling for reasoning'. Those children who come up from primary schools ready to explore personal experience aloud and to offer anecdotal contributions to discussion frequently cease to do so within a few weeks of arrival: they learn in certain lessons that anecdotes are held by the teacher to be irrelevant. It can be hypothesized that they begin to take part in each new 'subject' by taking in their teacher's behaviour as a reciprocal element in their own role as learners, so that his voice becomes one 'voice' in their own internal dialogues. Thus, because the teacher never asks questions that can be answered by anecdotes, anecdotes cease to be a part of their own thinking about the subject, and become 'unthinkable' as contributions to class discussion.

One of the more important qualifications to be made in retrospect relates to the model of the teacher that underlies the whole of this paper, and perhaps appears most clearly in the foregoing discussion of questions. It has been pointed out that in this essay I set up implicitly an idealized model of the teacher as one who single-mindedly pursues cognitive goals.[2] But teaching, the argument continues, is not like that: every teacher has to hold the attention and control the behaviour of a considerable number of young people who would often rather be elsewhere. For this reason, a realistic model of the teacher would have to acknowledge that he or she has to pursue goals of classroom control as well as of cognitive learning, and that if control is not achieved the teacher will have little opportunity to pursue the latter. This now seems to me a substantial and persuasive criticism. For example, the more difficulty a teacher has in managing a class the more questioning will be used not to advance thinking but simply to hold attention, and this can more readily be done by short, undemanding, 'closed' questions which demand attention by calling for a rapid succession of answers. Thus the patterns of questioning which we observed are as likely to be the result of the need to establish classroom control as the result of an unacceptable view of knowledge on the part of the teachers. Nevertheless, it is still true that any experienced teacher who finds himself or herself habitually adopting a pedagogy dominated by closed factual questions should be looking for alternative ways of holding attention. What I wrote in 1968 about the learning going on in some of these lessons still stands; particularly important is the exclusion of pupils from the formulation of ideas. But now the picture is complicated by understanding that some teachers may have allowed themselves to be trapped in a restrictive pedagogy by their fears of losing control of pupils, fears that may have been increased by the presence of a tape recorder.

Pupil Participation

A pupil's understanding of a new topic depends upon bringing what he or she knows already to bear upon it, since our ability to understand a message depends on the resources we bring to it. Meaning does not lie in words but in the cultural practices of those who use them. The possibility of pupils understanding what the teacher means is crucially dependent upon the availability of appropriate cultural resources which in part they already possess. The pedagogical problem in a room full of pupils is how to enable all of them to bring to mind relevant knowledge and understanding, and to 'recode'[3] it in terms of the new framework offered by the teacher. That is why pupils' participation in the formulating of ideas in speech or writing is of crucial importance, since this is the readiest means by which the teacher can ensure that their resources are brought to bear on the issue so that the new perspective can modify the old. It is this that justifies both our concern that so many questions were 'closed' (thus implicitly excluding pupils' existing understanding) and the wider emphasis upon participation.

It is not easy to measure pupil participation in lessons especially since it is the quality of participation which matters, rather than its vociferousness. Perhaps the main point can be made impressionistically: both of the teams of investigators, in 1966 and 1967, all of them experienced teachers, when asked what their sharpest impression of the materials had been, first mentioned 'passivity'. This is in spite of several very successful question-and-answer lessons, and two 1967 lessons in improvised drama and oral French (which have not been included in this analysis). Teachers talk far more than pupils can reply; and the reply time is shared amongst thirty or more pupils. Even if it were shared equally between them, none would have taken a large part in the day's *overt* activity. But this is no more than an impression;

it would not be impossible to believe that children were participating vividly but in silence. (Most passages quoted in this paper are chosen precisely because they show teacher–pupil interaction, so they may give the impression of more interaction than appears when the lesson is seen as a whole.)

In a paper published in 1977 Peter Woods[4] introduced the idea of teachers' 'survival strategies' such as 'negotiation' – obtaining a period of cooperation from pupils in exchange for time spent on a preferred activity; 'ritual' – keeping pupils busy with routine activities that are acceptable because intellectually undemanding; 'fraternization' – projects and lessons organized by pupils; and other strategies. Woods sees these as devices that enable teachers to accommodate to the conflict between high expectations, heavy demands and the resistance of uncooperative pupils. In my view he is assimilating strategies performing two different functions. At times he presents the strategies as substitutes for the true business of teaching, and this may be true of some of them: 'negotiation' and 'ritual', for example. But teaching and learning finally depend upon the collaboration of the learner. What he calls 'fraternization' and 'occupational therapy' are not merely means of control but tend to co-opt pupils' active participation in learning; they contribute valuably even to the learning of pupils whose examination-oriented efforts require no bribe or spur. Thus the assimilation of these into the category of 'survival strategies' misleadingly associates a restrictive pedagogy with alternative ways of managing pupils by conceding validity to their perspectives and involving them more actively in classroom communication. (This is not of course to deny that sometimes groups of older pupils become so disillusioned that they will not cooperate at all; such failure, however, provide no basis for general teaching policies.)

One of the most interesting questions raised by the material relates to the ways in which the teacher covertly signals to his pupils what their role as learners is to be. This has partly appeared above in the analysis of teachers' questions: in the 1967 sample, pupils are normally expected to reproduce information or reasoning, rather than to think for themselves. The 1966 lessons were not dissimilar. This question is reverted to in more detail in the subsections headed 'Thinking aloud' and 'Pupil-initiated sequences', but it is implicit throughout this section.

This section is subdivided into:

(a) The gulf between teacher and taught
(b) Thinking aloud
(c) Questioning to a predetermined end
(d) The teacher supplies a structure
(e) The demand for explicitness
(f) Pupil-initiated sequences

(a) *The gulf between teacher and taught*

What do we expect from classroom discussion? Frequently a teacher, through demonstration, exposition or textbook, presents an account of some aspect of the world and then by means of question and answer leads pupils to 'understand' this. 'Understanding' implies relating the new model of reality to the learners' existing model, modifying the latter in the process. Apart from rote memorizing, all learning takes place through changes in the learner's existing model of the world. In each classroom there are perhaps thirty learners, conceivably with thirty different ways of understanding the matter in hand. This is the central problem of teaching: how to enable thirty different processes of change to take place at the same time. What is required is the opportunity for pupils to try out their new understandings, to talk, make diagrams, write, calculate, so that the new modifies the old while at the same time the old plays its essential part in understanding the new. Let us look at some classroom discussions to see how far they are enabling at least some pupils to develop new understandings.

The teacher in Lesson F (1966; chemistry; grammar school) was explaining that milk is an example of the suspension of solids in a liquid:

T   You get the white . . . what we call casein . . . that's . . . er . . . protein . . . which is good for you . . . it'll help to build bones . . . and the white is mainly the casein and so it's not actually a solution . . . it's a suspension of very fine particles together with water and various other things which are dissolved in water . . .

P.1 Sir, at my old school I shook my bottle of milk up and when I looked at it again all the side was covered with . . . er . . . like particles and . . . er . . . could they be the white particles in the milk . . . ?

P.2 Yes, and gradually they would sediment out, wouldn't they, to the bottom . . . ?

P.3 When milk goes very sour it smells like cheese, doesn't it?

P.4 Well, it is cheese, isn't it, if you leave it long enough?

T   Anyway can we get on? We'll leave a few questions for later.

What is happening here? The teacher talks about milk, using his specialist language to help him perceive it as an exemplar of the category 'suspension', and to free him from all other contexts and categories it might appear in. But for his pupils 'milk' belongs not with 'suspension' but with 'cheese', 'school', 'shook', 'bottle'; they perceive it in that context and his use of 'casein' and 'fine particles' signals to only two of them that some different response is expected. Pupil 1 recognizes 'particles' and, searching his experience, comes up with lumps of curd. Trying to conform to the teacher's expectation, he manages 'the side was covered with . . . like particles', his uncertainty finding its expression in the deprecatory 'like'. Pupil 2 follows this line of thought and, associating the idea of sedimentation with suspended particles, tries 'they would sediment out'. These two pupils are beginning to use the language of science to make the specifically scientific abstraction from the experience. But Pupils 3 and 4, although they are *attentive to what the teacher appears to be saying*, are unable to make this abstraction; the words the teacher has used do not signal to them which aspects of the 'milk' experience should be abstracted. Far from helping them to bridge the gulf between his frame of reference and theirs, the teacher's language acts as a barrier, of which he seems quite unaware. They are left with their own first-hand experience – 'it smells like cheese'. The state of the other less articulate members of the class can only be guessed at. The teacher, frightened by his sudden glimpse of the gulf between them, hastily continues with the lesson he has planned.

This teacher teaches within his frame of reference; the pupils learn in theirs, taking in his words, which 'mean' something different to them, and struggling to incorporate this meaning into their own frames of reference. The language which is an essential instrument to him is a barrier to them. How can the teacher help his pupils to use this language as he does? Certainly not by turning away from the problem. By turning away from his pupils' half-understandings, the teacher is locating his task in his own preconceptions of a body of knowledge to be dealt with. 'Anyway can we get on?' expresses his sense of urgency at its bulk. But he is only partly right, for his task lies equally in those half-understandings, since upon them depends the possibility of his pupils ever grasping even part of that daunting bulk. By being excessively aware of knowledge as a corpus of authoritative statements and too little aware of knowledge as a person's struggle to understand the world, a teacher may debar some of his pupils from access to the very knowledge that he values so highly.

Beside this we may place a sequence from Lesson K (1967; history) in which the teacher, aware of the gulf between what the word 'language' means to him and to his pupils, attempts to bridge it.

T Now what do we mean by language?
P.1 The alphabet.
T That's part of it . . . what else?
P.2 How to speak.
T How to speak . . . yes . . . what else? . . . What else do you do with a language apart from speaking it?
P.3 Pronounce it.
T Well that's part of speaking . . . What else?
P.4 Learn how to say it.
T Still the same thing . . . yes?
P Sir, you can tell the countries by the language they speak.
T Yes, but what else can we use a language for? We don't always speak a language . . . I don't always speak a language when I want to get something over to someone who is not in the same room . . . probably a long way away . . . I can't shout or use the telephone . . . What do I do?
P Write.
T I write . . . right, therefore it's the written word as well as the spoken word.

Without the initial question the teacher is unlikely to have known how hard the pupils found it to conceive of language as a whole. He pursued the matter with some determination, but even at the end one does not know how far his references to the 'written word' and the 'spoken word' could mean anything to his pupils. He has, however, enabled a few pupils to take an active part in testing how far their meanings match with his.

Since most questions in the sample of lessons were closed-ended, pupils were seldom invited to think aloud, to generate new sequences of thought, to explore implications. If they were typical in this respect, teachers might well question their own attitudes and behaviour in the classroom. Are they teaching their younger pupils that to learn is to accept factual material passively and reproduce it for matching against the teacher's model, to be judged right or wrong? Should they reconsider their use of full class or small group discussion? It is in the give and take of reciprocal discussion that pupils can best try out new concepts and modify them in response to the teacher's replies.

Moreover it is important for the teacher to know whether the pupils are in a position to understand what he or she is telling them, or whether a wide gulf divides them. This information becomes available when pupils are encouraged to join in the thinking and to use what they have been taught, either orally or in writing. The disadvantage of writing for this purpose is that the teacher's reply is likely to be delayed, and that it is often restricted to a general comment or an assessment.

(b) *Thinking aloud*

At times teachers do try to involve pupils in exploring the subject:

(i) by requiring a pupil to 'think aloud', to generate a sequence of ideas for himself;
(ii) by discussion in which the teacher by questioning leads his pupils to a preconceived end;
(iii) by providing a linguistic structure for a pupil to complete.

These three will be the subject of this section and the following two. Examples of these categories are *very infrequent* and tend to involve only one child. For example, it is not easy in the twelve lessons to find occasions when pupils are required to think aloud. One occurs in Lesson G (1966; physics; comprehensive school). The teacher had put in front of the class a mechanism illustrating the working of an aneroid barometer. After a lengthy demonstration with explanations, the teacher asked about the function of part of the apparatus. A pupil replied:

> Well the silver knob is to turn that pointer ... If you turn that to say say twenty or whatever the other hand says ... when the other hand moves you can see the difference in pressure.

The pupil appears to understand how to use a barometer but to have some difficulty in formulating the process at the level of explicitness expected in a science lesson. In part the problem is a matter of linguistic forms: he lacks a general term such as 'the position of' to substitute for the phrase 'say twenty or whatever the other hand says'. It is clear that he understands the concept. But the problem also involves a failure in reflexive thought: for the account to be complete he needs to name an intermediate conceptual stage between setting the pointer and reading off the difference in pressure. This would give something like: 'From *the angle between* the two pointers, you can see'. An exchange like this gives the teacher some insight into pupils' understanding; further discussion would be required to encourage the pupil to re-analyse the process in order to discover what he had omitted. Telling him would not necessarily serve the purpose, since it would not be embedded in his own reflexive analysis of the process. This well illustrates a central pedagogical problem. Each pupil in the class is likely to have his or her own areas of incomprehension, vagueness and lack of reflection. How can a teacher give all of them adequate opportunities to explore and correct inadequacies? It can only be by teaching methods which include giving the initiative to the learners themselves within appropriate frameworks.

The physics lesson quoted above contained a number of similar examples of pupils thinking aloud, but these are infrequent in all other lessons in both years. This is partly related to the lack of open-ended questions, but questions which required pupils to reason about given material were also infrequent. The lack of open-ended questions may – it could be argued – arise from these young pupils' ignorance of the topic, which would delay their active participation to such time as they have an enabling knowledge. But this would not explain the lack of more limited questions, based upon given material, and requiring pupils at a simple level to operate the intellectual processes of the subject. This certainly happened in some mathematics lessons, but in general the pupils appeared to be 'learning' that learning is a passive receptive process. This may well make some of them unsatisfactory pupils at a later stage when more active participation is required of them.

In Lesson L (1967; physics) the pupils were asked to watch the behaviour of flames in a tin can into which gas was piped. (This was the lesson with thirty-two per cent open questions: the following is perhaps the most successful of the questions requiring interpretation of the teacher's demonstration.)

T Now when I turn the gas tap on . . . what's coming out of the top?
P Flames . . . luminous flames.
T What's coming out of the top of the tin?
P Um . . . air . . . that's been burnt . . . gas that's been burnt.
T Good. It's burnt gas . . . spare gas . . . so what's that tell you about the inside of the tin? . . . what is there inside there?
P Gas.
T It's full of gas, right . . . Now then, I'm going to turn off the gas and I want you to watch carefully . . . watch the flame and see anything . . . any change that you can . . . and also watch the tin carefully . . . Right, I shall turn it off. What did you see as soon as I turned it off?
P The flame went down.
T Why did it go down?
P Cos the . . . it wasn't . . . the gas wasn't coming for it to be burnt.
T There wasn't as much gas spare . . . we've burnt off the spare gas.

Here the teacher has succeeded in limiting the tasks so that it is quite explicit: the pupils do not have to guess at the criteria which she is using in judging the relevance of an answer. Yet the questions are relatively open-ended; they do little to constrict the language in which the child might answer (contrast for example the passage from Lesson

F about milk); they encourage the children to improvise explanations within the given frame of reference. It is worth noting that this teacher made it possible for pupils to pause and reshape their utterances: 'Cos the ... it wasn't ... the gas wasn't ...'

In Lesson N (1967; religious education) occurred an exchange which can be contrasted with this. The teacher was asking for the recall of information about life in New Testament Palestine.

T   How did they get the water from the well? ... do you remember? ... Yes?
P.1 They ... ran the bucket down ... er ... and it was fastened on to this bit of string and it ... [Here the words become inaudible for a phrase or two] ... other end to the water.
T   You might do it that way ... where did they put the water ... John?
P.2 In a big ... er ... pitcher.
T   Good ... in a pitcher ... which they carried on their ... ?
P   Heads.

The question 'How did they get the water from the well?' has signalled to Pupil 1 that this is a relatively open question to which an improvised sequence would be appropriate. His reply, the quality of which is here irrelevant, is met by, 'You might do it that way,' spoken with an intonation expressing doubt. That is, Pupil 1's answer is rejected, though in a polite form of words. Pupil 2 suggests an answer *of a different kind*; he intuits – or remembers – that his teacher does not want improvised reasoning but the name of an object. His reply, 'In a big ... er ... pitcher,' is accepted and carried further with a promptness which signals *to both pupils* that this is what was required in the first place. It might be surmised that these pupils are not only learning about Palestine but also about the kinds of reciprocal behaviour appropriate to a teacher–pupil relationship, that is, learning when not to think. (It should be remembered that they are in their sixth week in a new school.)

This is an example of the kind of question which the investigators came to call a 'pseudo-question', in that while it has the form of an open question the teacher's treatment of replies shows that he or she is willing to accept only one answer.

(c) Questioning to a preconceived end

Teachers who try to deal directly with sequences of thought may involve themselves in other problems. In Lesson E (1966; biology; comprehensive school) the teacher was recapitulating material previously taught:

T How does the fish obtain the oxygen from the water? What happens ... ? Stephen?
P It allows the water to run over its gills and the ... er ... and extracts the oxygen.
T First of all think of it in stages, Stephen. Where does the water go first of all?
P Miss, it enters the mouth and then it passes over the gills taking out the oxygen. Then it comes out of the gills.
T Comes out of the back of the gill-cover ...

The difficulty for the pupil seems to arise not only from the nature of the subject-matter. If he were explaining this to an equal for a given purpose, his choice of items would be determined by that purpose and the extent of his knowledge. But he is explaining this to a teacher who already knows it, and for an unstated purpose, so he can only construct a criterion for choosing items by projecting himself into the teacher's mind, partly in response to her signals of acceptance or rejection. The teacher seems to be demanding more specific references; the problem for the pupil must be to determine what will be relevant and acceptable – by what criteria the teacher is judging relevance. Once he has made these (usually unspoken) criteria his own he will be able to join in the teacher's mode of thought. Why, for example, should he specify 'the back of the gill-cover' since he has not specified 'the front of the mouth'? (It is worth noting how the pupil has searched for 'extracts the oxygen' after an abortive start 'and the ...' on a different formulation. He has already internalized some of his teacher's criteria.)

A carefully guided argument can be valuable when the pupil is on the point of comprehending the teacher's criterion, and can lead to the sudden jump of insight needed. In Lesson M (1967; English) the teacher is aiming to sharpen his pupils' awareness of traditional verse-scansion; a pupil has read aloud a limerick she has written

T 'Then to his surprise' ... yes?

P 'He slowly began to rise'.

T 'He slowly began to rise' ... We've got too many haven't we? Di dee didi dee ... Then we could really do with 'He ...'?

P 'He began to rise'.

T 'He began to rise' ... but it's not very good, is it? There's too many in it ... You've got to ...

P 'He *started* to rise'.

T 'He started to rise' ... that's better ...

The pupil's heavy emphasis on the first syllable of 'started' shows that she has taken in the teacher's criterion. (One wonders what would have happened if she had been asked to make her discovery explicit.) Sequences resulting in a flash of insight are infrequent. This is the only undoubted case in the material.

In the 1967 mathematics lesson (J) the proportion of reasoning questions to factual questions was 17:36, yet of these only nine were categorized as 'open'. The teacher was giving very closely-defined reasoning tasks and on the whole requiring pupils to take only one step at a time. This has been true of the two 1966 mathematics lessons also.

The next example shows that even in mathematics this may at times narrow the teacher's perception of the teaching possibilities. The teacher in Lesson J was requiring her pupils to operate the concepts of fractions by dividing rectangles into parts. She had prepared a large diagram to illustrate $\frac{3}{6} = \frac{1}{2}$:

She put this on show and told the class to divide a half into sixths. After a pause she picked up one boy's work (see diagram on next page):

T Why aren't I very happy with that one? ... I can't get cross and say it's wrong but I'm not happy ... [pause]

Come on ... think of what I asked you to do ... Linda?

P.1 You told us not to shade the second one but put in the number of sixths.

[A rectangular diagram divided into a 3×2 grid, with the top-left cell, top-middle cell, and bottom-left cell shaded and each labelled $\frac{1}{6}$]

T Oh no nothing like that ... You had to shade in the same areas as a half ... Well, has he shaded in the same area?

Ps [replies are inaudible]

T What's his shape ... what's his shape? ... What's it like?

P.2 He's just put two on the top and one on the bottom.

T Right ... well, it's like a fat L or something he's drawn ... It's right, isn't it Shaw?

P.3 Yes Miss.

T No, so it doesn't illustrate our point.

It did however show that some pupils – the boy whose diagram was being discussed, and Pupil 1, Linda – had not understood what they were doing. In this sequence the teacher does not make explicit either what the task is, or how it is that the boy's diagram 'doesn't illustrate our point'. Moreover, this might have seemed a useful opportunity to demonstrate that:

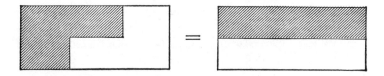

This possibility seems to have been concealed from her by the thoroughness of her prepared plan.

An enormous amount of talk washes over pupils in lessons. Their problem must be to select from it those utterances which make explicit the criteria by which their performances will be judged. Some teachers mark these utterances with different intonation patterns and vocal quality. When teachers do not do this, pupils must be faced with a difficult problem of selective attentiveness. It seems that some children so largely fail to perceive the nature of the given tasks that they are in effect not solving problems but copying external models; Linda may be one of these children, and so may a child (not quoted above) whose attention seemed to be directed to the colour of the shading. On the other hand, the boy whose diagram was criticized had been solving a spatial problem, even though its terms were not those given by the teacher. The teacher must find herself divided between clarifying tasks so that they can be comprehended by the first two, and following up issues raised by the latter. Preliminary planning helps with the former, but obscures the latter.

(d) Teacher supplies structure

The plight of children who have difficulty in making reasoning explicit can be helped by a method some teachers use, apparently without being aware of it.

Several examples occur in Lesson G (1966; physics comprehensive school). Of all the teachers whose lessons we have studied this teacher showed himself most aware of the gulf between his frame of reference and that of his pupils, and devoted his very considerable teaching skill to enabling his pupils to join in his own way of thinking and talking. Having talked about air pressure in terms of a model barometer, he moves out into other applications of the same ideas, first to 'spacemen' and then – in the course of the passage quoted below – to 'mountaineers'. (Several sentences identifying mountaineers have been omitted from the middle of the passage.)

T He carries an air supply because ... ? Why does he need an air supply?
P There isn't any air.
T Good. There isn't any air ... Where there's no air ... come on, complete it ... well?
P Life.
T If you've got no air you've got no ... ?
P Air pressure.

T No air pressure ... So what must mountaineers do if they find there's no
  air pressure?
  [three sentences omitted here]
T The reason why they want to have air cylinders is because ... ?
P There isn't any air, sir.
T Good. There isn't much air.

Here the teacher supplies the linguistic structure that represents causal
or other links between statements, and the pupils are required to have
so far followed the teacher's reasoning as to be able to supply one
statement of the linked pair. This seems particularly relevant to the
teaching of rational sequences which the teacher wishes to hand over
in a predetermined form.

Although requiring children to fill the gaps in a structure controlled
by the teacher may give them some familiarity with the rational
processes involved, we can surmise that its value for advancing understanding is limited. It is a powerful device for classroom control: by
such questions a teacher can hold the attention of a class and focus it
upon the intended sequence of statements. Equally the teacher can use
it as a source of information about individual pupils' ability to follow
the sequence of thought. It makes no allowance, however, for the
possibility that pupils may supply appropriate phrases without having
grasped the thinking that justifies them. Because it makes many major
choices for the pupils instead of requiring them to make them, it is
likely to be ineffective in making underlying principles available
to learners: in general it focuses upon the surface of an acceptable
performance, rather than upon the understanding from which that
performance should spring. Clearly it is a powerful tactic in the
teacher's repertoire, particularly for controlling attention, but it should
be used with full awareness of its limitations. In later pages I discuss
the difference between exploratory and presentational talk; questions
like those illustrated above will lead only to presentational answers. If
we want discussion in lessons to affect pupils' understanding – so
that on another occasion they can think out a similar problem for
themselves – they will have to engage in exploratory talk or writing.
Our competencies often show themselves in performance which is
controlled intuitively, but if we wish to be able to control or change

our performance we need to be consciously aware of it. And we become aware of performance by representing it to ourselves, either through language or through other symbolic systems.

(e) Demand for explicitness

It is now appropriate to move away from the teacher's duty to make publicly explicit to his pupils the criteria he is using. We now consider the function for the pupil of asking him to spell out explicitly what he is doing, thinking and learning. In effect, we are asking whether our material gives any evidence of what value it is to a pupil to express in words whatever it is that he or she is to learn. 'Knowing' can mean anything from being able to tick the right item in a multiple-choice question to being able to use whatever has been learnt to generate new insights. And in any new piece of learning it seems likely that the pupil has to make some progress along this continuum of understanding. For example, in mathematics the pupils need to progress from being able to carry out a process to being able to make the process itself the subject of their perception. (This seems to be related to Piaget's 'concrete' and 'formal' operations.) To find means of representing a process to oneself is to bring it under conscious control.

Something of this can be seen in a sequence from Lesson A (1966; second-year mathematics; grammar school).

T One divided by a quarter ... what does that mean? Somebody express that in everyday language.

P Quarter of one.

T Is it a quarter of one? What's a quarter of one?

P A quarter.

T A quarter. It's not going to be more than that? What is it then? Yes, Farley?

P Sir, it's one plus a quarter.

T It's what?

P One plus a quarter.

T That is one plus a quarter is it? [writing on blackboard] I thought *that* was one plus a quarter. And that?

P Sir.

T What's this one? ... What's it mean? Yes ... ?

P One divided by a quarter.

T It's one divided by a quarter. What does one divided by a quarter mean? Yes...?

P How many quarters are there in one.

T How many quarters are there in one. Well, if you think of it like that, 'How many quarters are there in one?' How many quarters *are* there in one? Yes, Brooke?

P Four, sir.

T Yes, there are four.

These pupils, a year older than the others, are being asked not merely to operate the process of division by fractional numbers, but to become aware of the process. By asking pupils to distinguish $1 + \frac{1}{4}$ from $1 \div \frac{1}{4}$, and to explain in other words the meaning of 'one divided by a quarter' he is encouraging his pupils – who have already added, multiplied and divided fractions – to make the process of division itself the object of their attention, and to distinguish it from the other processes.

There is a wide gap of understanding between the pupil who offered, 'One plus a quarter,' and the other who was able to say, 'How many quarters are there in one.' The teacher, however, accepts this latter contribution as the climax of the instructional sequence: he has made a 'right answer'; the point has been 'made'. Similarly in other lessons, the one child's answer is allowed to represent an achieved end, when the teacher can hardly know whether other pupils have reached the same level of comprehension. For example, in Lesson B (1966; mathematics; secondary modern) the teacher who is introducing the idea of co-ordinates, asks the class to draw the diagram on p. 42. Then he establishes by questions that when x is 2, then y is 2, and so on. Finally he asks: 'Can anybody tell me how I can write that down on the blackboard in a kind of shorthand way?' and when one pupil replies, 'x equals y' treats this as clinching the sequence.

In both of these cases the teacher was asking children to verbalize very abstract processes, and this was clearly very valuable to part of the class, at the very least. What is also worthy of note is the teacher's need for a climactic explicitness before he can leave the sequence. These examples demand the question: if one child benefits from making the conclusion explicit, would not others? This generates a practical problem, however. Can a teacher facing thirty different children devise

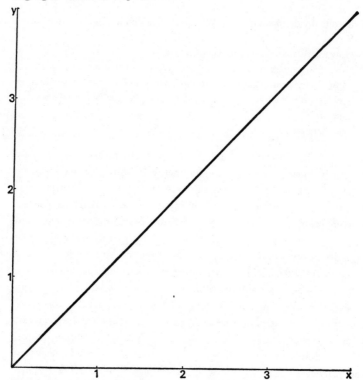

ways of enabling all of them to make explicit their understanding, in order to increase their awareness of the process they are engaged in? It is difficult but not impossible.

A quite different kind of explicitness was sought by the teacher of Lesson D (1966; geography; girls' grammar school). The class was looking at a photograph of sand dunes.

T   Sand dunes. They're usually in an unusual ... a specific shape ... a special shape ... Does anybody know what shape they are? Not in straight lines ...

P   They're like hills.

T   Yes, they're like low hills.

P   They're all humpy up and down.

T   Yes, they're all humpy up and down.

P   They're like waves.

T Good, they're like waves.

P They're like . . .

T They're a special shape.

P They're like boulders . . . sort of go up and down getting higher and higher.

T I don't know about getting higher and higher.

P Something like pyramids.

T Mm . . . wouldn't call them pyramids, no.

P They're in a semi-circle.

T Ah, that's getting a bit nearer. They're often in a semi-circle and nearly always . . . we call them . . . well, it's part of a semi-circle . . . What do we call part of a semi-circle? You think of the moon . . . perhaps you'll get the shape.

P Water.

T No, not shaped like water . . . Yes?

P An arc.

T An arc . . . oh, we're getting ever so much nearer.

P Crescent.

T A crescent shape. Have you heard that expression . . . a crescent shape? I wonder if anybody could draw me a crescent shape on the board. Yes, they're nearly all that shape . . .

Although the teacher seems from the first to have been looking for the verbal label, 'crescent', in the course of searching for it language was used in quite other ways than in merely offering a series of labels for rejection or acceptance. At first the girls, who had a picture (and probably some personal experience) to start from, took the question as an invitation to *make this experience explicit*. Thus we have 'like hills', 'like waves', 'sort of go up and down getting higher and higher', and the strikingly evocative 'all humpy up and down'. They are not taking the shared experience of shape as given and finding a name for it; they are exploring *what meaning any agreed name should have*. But 'like pyramids' turns the class towards the labelling function of language, so that 'in a semi-circle', having earned the teacher's approval, directs the class towards 'arc' and 'crescent'.

It could be said that the classroom dialogue was being used for different purposes by teacher and class. The teacher wanted not merely the shape but a precise word, 'crescent', and pursued this goal through the method sometimes known as 'focusing'.[5] No amount of analytical thought would enable a pupil who did not already know the answer 'crescent' to work it out for herself. Thus they can only show themselves to be 'good pupils' by a submissive attentiveness to the teacher's clues. But at the beginning most pupils who spoke were not playing that game but the different one of using the photograph as evidence and trying to describe their shapes as precisely as possible, a far more rational activity. (The teacher also failed to notice that her pupils were describing dunes as they were shown from one side in the photograph, whereas she was thinking of their shape as seen from above. One wonders how often pupils' apparently irrational replies – 'Water,' for example – would become rational if viewed from another perspective.)

Would the class have gained as much if the name 'crescent' had come as an immediate answer to the first question? What did they gain? Why were there so few occasions in the twelve lessons when pupils were asked to observe and to describe precisely what they had observed? Does this represent a significant lack in the learning experience of younger secondary pupils, or is this merely a chance bias of the small sample? What function has language like 'all humpy up and down' for the child who used it? Is it the vestige of something to be outgrown, or the unformed promise of something to come? This single example can raise these questions but not answer them.

(f) *Pupil-initiated sequences*

When another adult gives us new information we may or may not question him. This seems to be determined by our assessment of the role we are playing at that moment, and especially by our role-relationship with the speaker. One would therefore expect that in the classroom, where the pupil's role as learner and the teacher's role as mediator are so well defined, questioning of the teacher by the pupils would take a large part of lesson time, side by side with presentation and application activities. Yet any teacher knows that this is not so. Why, then, do our pupils not actively ask questions that would help bridge the gulf between their frame of reference and that of the teacher?

In investigating those occasions when pupils played an active role in initiating a new aspect of the topic, we included only cases where a pupil had of his own accord raised a new issue, either by an unsolicited statement, or by a question. This definition of 'pupil-initiated sequences' made it possible to separate out twenty examples from the twelve lessons. These included:

3 requests for information for its own sake
4 requests for information to confirm an insight
1 request for a theoretical explanation
6 questions about the method of carrying out a task
6 statements

———

20 total

———

The questions about practical methods are different in kind from the others. 'Can we use *deep* pencil?' (i.e. heavy shading) for example, seemed to be a request for reassurance rather than information. However, such requests for advice give important information to teachers and investigators alike by displaying pupils' uncertainty about how much initiative they are expected to take.

The requests for information fall into two parts: some appear to be merely fact gathering. The teacher has taught a coherent body of facts, but the pupil has perceived them as separate, and is asking for more. But other requests for information show that a pupil has gained an insight and wishes to test it; in two cases these insights were not revelant to what the teacher was teaching. What the teacher teaches is not the same as what the pupil learns. All of the six 'statements' were sharply relevant, and in two cases they corrected errors made by teachers.

So perhaps nine of these sequences show pupils engaging in learning as actively as intelligent adults do. This is so minute a part of the total time of the twelve lessons as to challenge further attention.

The Language of Instruction

In this section we turn aside from *how* language is used by teachers and their pupils in order to consider *what* language they use, and the implications of this for learning. That is, our attention will be given to forms rather than functions. We can take guidelines from a paper about 'The Problems of Impersonal Language' which Harold Rosen wrote in 1966:[6]

> ... the verbalization of concepts within different subjects has a complex history; it is probably not a simple matter of perfectly evolved language which embodies one kind of rational thought. The models we look at are social institutions, and the differences between say the language of geology and the language of history may be in part due to the different history of these two subjects. In all events we should set about distinguishing between the linguistic-conventional and the linguistic-intellectual, so that we can understand that traditional formulations are not sacrosanct.

Having thus questioned the functions of subject-specific linguistic registers, Professor Rosen in a later passage looked at some of their implications for learning:

> Much of the language encountered in school looks at pupils across a chasm. Some fluent children ... adopt the jargon and parrot whole stretches of lingo. Personal intellectual struggle is made irrelevant and the personal view never asked for. Language and experience are torn asunder. Worse still, many children find impersonal language mere noise. It is alien in its posture, conventions, and strategies ... These are extremes. Many children have areas of confidence and understanding but frequently have to resort to desperate mimicry to see them through.

In discussing the language used by teachers in the recorded lessons we were concerned not only with stylistic characteristics but with their awareness of the language forms they used and their presentation of them to pupils. We were concerned with the effect of teachers' language upon pupils' participation in learning in the manner that Harold Rosen suggested. Was the teachers' language acting as an induction into new styles of thought and communication or was it setting up barriers? We found it useful to separate three aspects of teachers' language:

(a) *Specialist language presented.* This includes language forms special to the teacher's subject which he or she is aware of as a potential barrier to his pupils' understanding, and therefore 'presents' to them with deliberate care.

(b) *Specialist language not presented.* Language forms special to the subject may not be deliberately 'presented' to pupils either (i) because they have previously been introduced, or (ii) because the teacher is not aware of using them. (Since the samples were taken in the sixth week of the pupils' secondary education examples of the latter are likely to be far more numerous.)

(c) *The language of secondary education.* This phrase is used here to refer to a loose cluster of styles including the style in which textbooks are usually written, the style of substantial magazine and newspaper articles, the style in which weighty public topics are discussed. Such styles are more often written than spoken, except in schools and colleges: the style in which this book is written would undoubtedly fall within this category. The point of isolating such a loose cluster is that even when it does not include technical terms, the style as a whole is resistant to anyone who is not familiar with it.

(a) *Specialist language presented*

It would not be true to say that teachers are unaware that language plays a part in learning. The eleven teachers in the sample were sharply aware of certain aspects of the language they used – and to some extent expected their pupils to use – in managing their subject matter. It is important to notice the unanimity with which teachers perceive certain specialist terms and fail to perceive the rest of the language they used; the study demonstrated this beyond doubt.

Teachers are aware of certain of the technical terms they use, showing this by what we shall call 'presenting' the terms. 'Presentation' will sometimes imply that a term is supplied by the teacher and a definition asked for, and at other times that the teacher explicitly gives a name, or asks pupils to give a name, to a concept which has already been established. (In the sample, the pupils were asked to supply a term or a definition three times as often as the teacher supplied them.) For example, in Lesson F (chemistry; grammar school) the words 'chromatography', 'pestle and mortar', 'suspension', 'effluent' and 'chlorophyll' were presented to the class. Examples were much less

47

common in the lessons from non-selective schools, with the sole exception of Lesson K (history) which presented 'city states', 'patriotic', 'inquiring mind', 'language', 'truce', and 'pentathlon'. It will be noted that these are mainly nouns. Neither in science nor maths lessons could a systematic policy be perceived, either in the selection of concepts to be taught or in the order of presentation of the concept and a term to represent it.

Indeed, in many of the twenty-five examples examined it is hard to say what value could come either from defining a term or in providing a term for a concept which pupils had already verbalized successfully. An extreme case occurred in Lesson F:

T We're going to cut the grass into small pieces and then we're going to put it into the ... what we call a mortar ... this is what we call a mortar ... this bowl ... and anyone know what we call the other thing which we're going to pound it in?

The act of giving a technical name seems for many teachers to have taken on a value of its own in separation from its utility; in this case the naming activity is totally irrelevant to the process which it interrupts.

Later in the same lesson the teacher, his attention upon name teaching, fails to notice a pupil whose reply shows his incomprehension:

T Now I don't know whether any of you could jump the gun a bit and tell me what actually is this green stuff which produces green colour ...
P Er ... um ... water.
T No ... Have you heard of chlorophyll?

The pupil's reply should have warned the teacher that there were children in the class to whom he was communicating nothing. (When seen in the total context of the lesson, the child's reply must mean no less than this.) In this case, the teacher's desire to teach terminology prevents him from perceiving his pupils' needs as learners.

In Lesson E (1966; biology; comprehensive school) also, the biological terminology seems to take a value of its own:

T Where does it go then?

48

P To your lungs, Miss.

T Where does it go before it reaches your lungs? . . . Paul.

P Your windpipe, Miss.

T Down the windpipe . . . Now can anyone remember the other word for windpipe?

P The trachea.

T The trachea . . . good . . . After it has gone through the trachea where does it go to them? . . . There are a lot of little pipes going into the lungs . . . what are those called? . . . Ian?

P The bronchii.

T The bronchii . . . that's the plural . . . What's the singular? What is one of these tubes called? . . . Ann.

P Bronchus.

T Bronchus . . . with 'us' at the end . . . What does 'inspiration' mean . . . ?

This too is an extreme case, which underlines an assumption shared in some degree by six of the twelve teachers; the teaching of terminology is seen as part of the task. It is clear from the substitution of 'trachea' for 'windpipe' that it is not merely the referential function of the word that is valued; the teacher is valuing that of the two synonyms which carries with it (for her, not the pupils, of course) the stronger suggestion of a strictly biological context.

It has been pointed out that our literacy-oriented culture induces us to assume that meaning is a characteristic of words rather than a cultural attribute of the people who use those words.[7] This may account for the excessive value given by some teachers to the mere recognition of words by their pupils.[8] As the exchanges quoted show, this can at worst shroud from teachers' gaze the meanings which provide the only valid justification for teaching the words. The words without the concepts they represent in adult use are strictly useless to pupils. As their grasp of a concept develops, the technical term becomes a useful centre about which can cluster relevant experiences and understanding; presented too soon the term may actually inhibit the process of clustering and abstraction. It is a delicate pedagogical choice when the use of a technical term becomes helpful rather than the reverse. The intention in this passage is not to suggest that science (or other) teachers should not teach standard terminology but to warn them that some of their emphasis on terms appears to an observer to be counter-productive.[9]

Some teachers find a greater propriety in the familiar specialist term. The teacher of religious knowledge in Lesson N (1967) said men pray to God 'because God controls the earth ... because he controls the weather ... so that the food can grow that we are able to have it ... God *provides* ... is the word ... God provides this food for us ...' When he said, '*provides* ... is the word', he was claiming the authority not only to inform his pupils about Christian theology but also to determine the language by which the theological concepts are to be represented. 'Provides' no doubt carried important associations for him; it is less likely to do so for eleven-year-old children. It seems, when he insisted on its propriety, that he was assuming that these meanings lie within the word itself.

Two examples of presentation have been quoted above in the section on 'pupil participation': a discussion of the shape of sand-dunes leading to the presentation of 'crescent' (p. 42), and the investigation of the meaning for the pupils of the word 'language' (p. 30) in which their use of the term limited it to spoken language. The latter was quoted as an example of valuable classroom discussion; very few of the other twenty-four examples of presentation could be quoted approvingly for that purpose. The technical term is often taken to have a value of its own, and its substitution for an alternative formulation is sometimes taken to have the weight of an explanation.

(b) Specialist language not presented

The range of technical language (that is, language special to a curricular subject) of which teachers are sufficiently aware to present in this way is limited, as will have been seen. Side by side with these presentations, some teachers are using specialist language without explicitly presenting it.

Some of these were technical terms of the subject: in an English lesson 'stress' and 'rhyme'; in physics 'diagram' and 'pulley'; in mathematics 'point'; in history 'a major city'. Others were as much part of the teacher's idiolect as part of the subject register; one mathematics teacher used 'split' repeatedly, whereas another used 'sliced' and 'divided' in similar contexts. (Mathematics lessons appear to have a register of their own, quite separate from the register of mathematics proper.) With these might be classed 'pointer' (physics), 'an unhappy ending' (English), and others.

Technical language was most pervasive in the chemistry lesson (F) recorded in a boys' grammar school; we have already quoted the passage in which a teacher tries to explain that milk is 'a suspension of very fine particles together with water'. Almost every sentence contains similar subject-specific terms. A more extreme example is:

> T Put that into the distillation flask and then distil off and then we get a thermometer recording the correct temperature which is the boiling point for acetone. Then we collect the acetone which came over as a distillate.

This teacher showed that he had difficulty in talking of his subject without using its terminology. In the passage quoted below he wishes to say that it would be possible to extract all the colour from grass by using a more complex form of his method, but was unable to free himself from the phrase 'under reflux conditions' enough to realize that he had already said enough with 'using a different method'.

> T If we did it using a different method actually . . . where we heat up the grass with acetone actually . . . heating it under, er . . . an enclosed system except . . . I'll have to show using a diagram on that . . . well er . . . under reflux conditions so that we didn't lose the acetone then we could actually finish up with the grass a white colour.

It can be surmised that this teacher's enthusiasm for his subject and his abundance of knowledge tended to stop him from perceiving his pupils' needs. Talk of this kind would certainly discourage many pupils; it is tempting to make guesses about which pupils would be best able to tolerate such language and to continue to attend to it until such time as they could begin to take part. It was shown above (p. 29) that at least two boys were beginning to be able to take part. For these two, the dialogue with the teacher must have been exciting; for the others it is likely to have been a painful demonstration of their inadequacy.

It is important to consider the issues raised by such teaching in terms not of 'learning language' nor of 'extending vocabulary' but of giving or withholding access to the conceptual framework of a subject. As teachers introduce central concepts and their conventional names, what is important is that pupils should meet 'concept-and-term' in a wide enough range of contexts of use to enable them to grasp its internal complexity and limits of use. Yet 'meet' itself is misleading, since they are more likely to relate the new term to their existing understanding if they are using it themselves in contexts which give them feedback, that is in discussions with the teacher and with one another. Thus the teacher of biology (Lesson E) was giving her pupils greater access to thinking in her subject by involving pupils in exchanges which required them to express the concepts of her subject. The technical terms when they occurred were defined implicitly by the context. The pupils of the chemistry teacher, on the other hand, might come to recognize the words he used but had restricted opportunity to grasp their meaning. Understanding, however, is not a matter simply of knowing the meaning of a word or not knowing it. Our understanding of a concept is capable of lengthy development: consider for example the long conceptual journey of a child's grasp of 'energy' to his or her understanding of it twenty years later as a research physicist. Nor is it a matter of a single word: 'energy' is to be understood in relation to a network of other concepts. This development of meaning, which can in principle continue throughout our lives, depends on use, and particularly on use in contexts which supply feedback.

(c) *The Language of Secondary Education*

The cluster of stylistic variations called here 'the language of secondary education' includes those one would expect to find in textbooks, in official publications and indeed in most printed documents which set out to discuss public topics in an impersonal manner. It also includes many of the styles to be found in public debate, in committee meetings and in academic lectures, though one often has the sense that originally written styles are being adapted to spoken use. Martin Joos called this 'the consultative style'.[10] It seems more appropriate to refer to it as a cluster of styles rather than as a 'register', which suggests a much more uniform set of characteristics which might be open to relatively tight definition. All men and women who wish to take a full part in social life need a command of explicit public language. What is in question is the part that varieties of this language should play in the classroom at different stages.

An attempted analysis (into the three categories: Specialist language presented; Specialist language not presented; The language of secondary education) of the language used in some of these lessons quickly made it clear that the relationship of one category to another could not be expressed in numerical terms. The language of secondary education was not just a matter of unfamiliar words that could be counted; nor did any other objective unit offer itself. It was necessary to fall back upon a subjective impression supported by examples. In the lessons from non-selective schools, specialist terms, presented or not, were infrequent; most of the teachers, however, used many terms which, while not specialist, would not be part of the language of their pupils' everyday living. Lessons from selective schools were even more dominated by this language of secondary education, as even a cursory reading showed.

This implies that if we speak of 'the language of history lessons' or of 'the language of physics lessons' we are more likely to be considering forms of language which are shared by these than forms which are specific to one or other of them. But it is not this dominant style of language which teachers are aware of; rather teachers perceive the specialist terms which they 'present'. It follows that they are not taking responsibility for their use of this style, and are unaware of any problems which its use may add to their pupils' tasks in learning.

Another way of looking at this style, then, is to see it as including those non-specialist forms of language which are outside the normal experience of eleven-year-old pupils. The linguistic experience of eleven-year-olds must, however, vary so much that this formulation is of little use except to emphasize that a lesson largely couched in such language will be beyond many pupils' comprehension.

We illustrate a teacher's unawareness of the language of secondary education from Lesson K (1967); the teacher, who is not a history specialist, used the phrase 'city states', paused, and then defined it:

> T They were called 'city states' because they were complete in themselves ... They were governed by themselves ... ruled by themselves ... they supported themselves [short omission] ... These states were complete in themselves because the terrain between cities was so difficult that it was hard for them to communicate ... Now because these people lived like this in their own cities they tended to be intensely patriotic towards their own city ... Now what's 'patriotic' mean?

What is notable here is not so much an obvious blunder such as 'terrain' but that in trying to explain 'city states' the teacher seems unable to escape from language equally unfamiliar to children: 'complete in themselves', 'ruled by themselves', 'supported themselves', 'communicate', 'tended to be'. 'City states' is typical of the kind of concept which teachers are enough aware of to 'present' to pupils; the other phrases exemplify the language of secondary education, which this teacher was so unaware of that he used it to explain the former. It is not until he reaches 'patriotic' that he recognizes another concept which needs presentation. Concepts such as 'complete in themselves' or 'tended to be' may carry less meaning to the child than does 'patriotic', which can easily be linked with something he knows. One set of counters is being substituted for another; words are being shown to be equivalent to words; and it is left to the pupils to summon up some kind of meaning for them. In learning such essential concepts as 'tendency', which form part of no specialism, the child is given no support from school, which tacitly assumes that he comprehends them. Children whose home life does not support such language learning may feel themselves to be excluded from the conversation in the classroom.

Any group that meets frequently for work or play develops a language style of its own. This will only partly be comprised of technical terms needed for the shared activity; there is likely to be an 'in-group' way of putting things, cryptic because of shared assumptions and experience, comfortable for insiders but likely to rebuff and discourage outsiders. Each one of us takes part in several of these groups, in the family, at work, at clubs and sports, and so on; membership of each group carries with it competence in using group language. Harold Rosen's separation of the 'linguistic-conventional' from the 'linguistic-intellectual' in specialist language (see p. 46) led me to distinguish between the *socio-cultural* functions of speech, which serve to indicate the speaker's role, group-membership and relationship with listeners, and the *conceptual* functions which are concerned with thinking about the subject:

Socio-cultural. A specialist linguistic style serves to remind speaker (and listener) that he or she is speaking as a physicist (perhaps) or more generally as a scientist, or as a committee member, or a participant in a public meeting. The style helps to maintain this temporary identity, and perhaps to hold at the centre of our attention this particular mode of understanding the world, in contrast with the other modes at our disposal. This function is essentially social, concerned with sustaining the cultural identity relevant at that moment in that situation.

Conceptual. This refers to the function we are all aware of, the exchange of messages about a subject-matter, and also the heuristic function, the use of language as a means of reflecting upon and reordering our understanding of a topic. However, the very same words that embody these functions may at the same time implicitly propose a view of what the social relationships between participants are: socio-cultural and conceptual functions are normally performed by one and the same utterance. Thus, when in the following paragraphs, phrases are attributed to one function or the other, what is being referred to is the dominant function in that case.

Difficulties arise when we apply these two categories to the phrases used in the sample of lessons. Certain cases fall predominantly into the socio-cultural category:

'is still quite apparent today' (K)
'The point I would like to make is' (L)
'prepare the evening meal' (N)
'from exhaustion' (G)

If these were phrased differently ('because they were tired' for 'from exhaustion'), this would not alter that part of the meaning which relates to the subject matter, but only that part which relates to the speaker's attitude to his present role.

Other cases fall into the conceptual category:

'a civilization . . . better developed' (K)
'something in common' (M)
'present together in that proportion' (L)
'the position of . . . in relation to . . .'(B)

These differ in that, *for the speaker*, a change in the terminology would be a change in that part of the meaning which relates to the subject matter. But *for most pupils* the phrases would not have this precise meaning; the precise relationships implied in 'developed', 'in common', 'proportion', and 'relation' would be likely to carry a far more *generalized* significance for them. Thus, although the two categories properly describe aspects of the teacher's *production* of these utterances, the pupils may be receiving all of them as socio-cultural in nature. These considerations should be kept in mind during the discussion which follows.

When the teacher asks 'How many pieces does that cake *consist of*?' is he using 'consist of' merely because it is habitual to his role of mathematics teacher, or does it remind him of certain assumptions about the possibility of numerical analysis of physical phenomena? Clearly in this case the conceptual content is latent: by using 'does that cake consist of' rather than 'has that cake been cut into' the teacher holds his own mental processes within a frame within which many latent mathematical concepts are available. For pupils, however, the situation is different. Each new item must first appear to have a socio-cultural function – that is, to be 'the sort of thing my physics teacher says' – and then, in so far as the pupil is able to use the item in talking, thinking or writing, it will take upon itself a conceptual function. We might ask ourselves by what processes a child becomes not only able to make his statements acceptable to the teacher as socially appropriate, but also internalize the teacher's conceptual frame so that what the pupil says means the same to him as it does to the teacher.

In all lessons in the sample the teacher's language at times showed some of the stylistic characteristics we are calling 'the language of secondary education'. This style was considerably more pervasive in lessons from selective schools, but even these showed considerable variation. In one degree or another, the style was accompanied by the technical terminology of a specialism, particularly in the physical sciences. The teacher in Lesson F (chemistry; grammar school) spoke throughout the lesson in the language of secondary education, using technical terms frequently. Other teachers slipped into the style only occasionally. Some teachers of arts subjects used almost no technical terms but carried out much of their presentation in the language of secondary education. For example, from Lesson C:

T The nature of the land together with the climate really controlled what was grown on Crete and what sort of occupations the people on the island performed.

Since this style is so pervasive it may well be a more important element in pupils' access to some subjects than the technical terms of those subjects.

The language of everyday social intercourse is, of course, a very powerful means of representing and organizing experience. In comparison, the strength of specialist subjects such as physics or economics is that they offer means of abstracting particular aspects of that experience so that they can be focused upon. Part of the business of secondary education is to make available to pupils those forms of discourse which support various ways of codifying experience. But a 'form of discourse' is not just a vocabulary and a style to be imitated: it is a way of understanding the world. Learning to codify experience in a new way is far more than learning new language forms. Any teacher knows of pupils who have learnt whole stretches of a new register which they can put together only in ways which demonstrate that they are not using the language as symbols for new dimensions along which to locate their experiences. Thus the teacher's task should not be to introduce a new set of linguistic forms, but to help his pupils to use language to organize experience in a new way.

The language of secondary education plays an ambiguous role in this. As the language in which the major concerns of our society are publicly discussed, its mastery is essential for full participation in adult life. Moreover, since it is the language of textbooks, teachers and lecturers, it is a necessary part of access to secondary education. But the culture of children's homes does not give them equal familiarity with these styles: compare, for example, the styles in which different newspapers are written. The sociologist Pierre Bourdieu has pointed out the importance of style in school success, though he refers not only to linguistic styles but also to other intangible preferences for content, attitudes and manner which influence teachers' judgements of pupils' work.[11] Moreover, if the language of secondary education predominates in a teacher's presentation it is likely to influence adversely some pupils' ability to identify their purposes with those of the teacher. The dilemma is not easily solved. If teachers are aware that the style they slip into so easily may present problems to their pupils, this should help them to choose intermediate styles which make gradual access possible. But a one-way presentation is not enough. Both for mastery of the style and mastery of the concepts active participation in discussion and in writing is essential: we discover the possibilities of what we can say and write by talking and writing.

Here lies the importance of pupil participation. It is when the pupil is required to use language to grapple with new experience or to order old experience in a new way that he is most likely to find it necessary to use language differently. And this will be very different from taking over someone else's language in external imitation of its forms: on the contrary, it is the first step towards new patterns of thinking and feeling, new ways of representing reality to himself. It is not enough for pupils to imitate the forms of teachers' language as if they were models to be copied; it is only when they 'try it out' in reciprocal exchanges so that they modify the way they use language to organize reality that they are able to find new functions for language in thinking and feeling. This would suggest that the low level of pupil participation in these lessons, if they are at all typical of secondary lessons, is a matter of some educational urgency. All teachers might well contemplate the classroom implications of this.

Douglas Barnes

Language and Classroom Control

Information from this study about the relationship between styles of language and styles of teacher–pupil interaction proved sparse. It may well be that a study such as this is not the best way of gathering such information. We are not primarily concerned with what most teachers would mean by 'controlling a class'. Classroom control is not a matter of reprimand and punishment: these only become necessary when control has broken down. Control is a matter of inducing pupils to give their serious attention to the matter in hand. It can be achieved in various ways, one of them being a rapid sequence of questions and answers. In their account of the language of teaching, Edwards and Furlong give a central place to what they call the teacher's 'shaping of meaning'. In their view, 'The pupil has to step into the teacher's system of meanings, which either confirms or extends or even replaces his own.'[12] It is towards this that the teacher's control of pupils' attention is steering them, though the phrase 'step into' oversimplifies the complex process of reconstructing the teacher's frame of reference from the pupils' existing resources at the bidding of clues let fall during lessons. Of course, control can be achieved by other methods than by a remorseless sequence of relatively simple questions, for example by co-opting the interests and purposes of the children into pursuing the topic of the lesson. In any case, control and the teaching of subject-matter are normally one and the same thing.

A teacher establishes his relationship with his pupils – their mutual expectations, that is – more in instructional sequences than in the small proportion of sequences overtly concerned with social control. Thus it is not enough to consider the relationship between language, teacher–pupil relationships and learning only in sequences which are overtly concerned with managing pupils' behaviour. The language of the teacher enacts for the child the relevance of the lesson. We have already quoted (on p. 42) a sequence from Lesson D in which the teacher allows her pupils, almost by accident, to explore with words the shape of sand dunes on the way to choosing 'crescent shape' to describe them. ('All humpy up and down', etc.) This teacher, though in general she used the language of secondary education, was also able to speak informally. 'Pop it in the oven', and 'Can't half make you jump', contrast notably with her usual lecturing style. Like several other teachers, she was aware how unfamiliar much of what she was teaching must seem to her pupils. On the whole she dealt with this by supplying an abundance of details, but upon several occasions she used familiar comparisons: 'It gets terribly hot during the day ... so hot that you could fry an egg on the rocks.' Speaking of marking tracks in a sand-desert she said:

T If you go from here to Manchester over the top road over the Pennines ... over the hills ... you'll find that across the roads ... um on the road ... along the roads there are poles put by the side of the road so that when the road is covered over with snow the tops of the poles remain above ... then you can find your way. Any of you seen the poles over the moors? Oh, some of you. Well, the same sort of thing happens in the desert ...

A similar sequence occurs in Lesson G (1966; physics; comprehensive school). Having demonstrated with apparatus that a greater weight of air above causes greater pressure in the air below, the teacher wishes his pupils to apply this to places they know.

T If I put three barometers ... one on top of Norland Moor, one at school ... and one right in the middle of Blackpool Promenade ... which one ... now you've got to think this out ... which one would go up the furthest because it's the biggest pressure ...?

For all its colloquial qualities this passage is extremely precise and well adjusted to its purposes. (Some teachers may disagree about its precision, but we should not allow this to divert attention from its function in helping the children to take part in the lesson.) The colloquial flexibility and informality of this teacher's style establishes a warm social interchange which invites pupils to contribute. By retaining something of the warmth and improvisatory quality of lively everyday speech, he encourages pupils to feel that what they can bring from their own lives is relevant to what is being talked about. They too can use language to grope for new meanings, to sort out experience for themselves. An important quality of a teacher's language is whether it is warm, exploratory, available, encouraging the child to involve himself actively in the learning, or whether it is cold, inflexible, defensive, and discouraging.

The Predominance of Language

In both 1966 and 1967 the investigators were surprised at the predominance of language in the lessons. In four mathematics lessons and one English lesson the blackboard was used, but in only one case (to be quoted below) was it used other than as an illustration of oral exposition. One maths teacher had prepared large diagrams on paper. In two physics lessons and one chemistry lesson the teacher demonstrated with apparatus, in all cases as the basis for a verbal exchange. Textbooks, including an atlas, were used in two history, one geography, and one religious education lesson; in the geography lesson a small picture in the book was discussed (see p. 42). That is, the study would suggest that 'chalk and talk' is still predominant in the classroom, except for one lesson. This is Lesson H, which for various reasons was not included in the analysis, and which was a drama lesson, taught in the school hall by the same teacher who taught Lesson M. This lesson consisted solely of individual or group improvisation; language entered only in the teacher's instructions, and the groups' discussion of their tasks.

In Lesson C (1966; history, grammar school) the teacher was seeking to give a picture of Minoan civilization. Well informed, and an exceptionally fluent speaker, she lectured to the class giving them what might be called 'word pictures'. Pupils played only a small part in her lessons.

T The artists on the island of Crete showed the things of nature as nearly as possible as they saw them ... When the Egyptian artists painted they made things rather still and formal and er an Egyptian artist would paint a flower but the flower wouldn't look as if it was growing. It would look as if it was cut out and still and stiff, whereas the Minoan artists showed a flower and you could almost feel that you could see it bending in the wind ... it was painted in a much more graceful and natural way ...

For all this teacher's vividness ('cut out and still and stiff') and flexible variation of intonation and vocal quality, one cannot but feel that this would have been better done with the aid of pictures, and by the pupils talking more than the teacher.

It is not difficult to point to several passages like this one in which the teacher's intentions could probably have been carried out more effectively if visual or other materials had been available. Yet this does not seem to exhaust the implications of the domination of lessons by language – and mainly by the teacher's spoken language it should be noted. The domination seems to amount to an unintended restriction of the kinds of learning which can go on in the classroom. Pupils could take a more active part in manipulating materials, in planning and carrying out demonstrations, and in measuring and recording what they perceive. This is not to denigrate the function of language in learning: indeed, in these lessons the failure to demand active involvement of the pupils *has gone hand in hand with a failure to demand that they verbalize their learning*, that is, that they use language as an active instrument for reorganizing their perceptions. It is not that there is too much language, but that it is not fulfilling its functions as an instrument of learning. Rather, *language is seen as an instrument of teaching*.

It has already been suggested that the blackboard can be used in two ways: it can be used to illustrate the teacher's verbal exposition; in subjects where the matter taught can be represented upon a plane surface, it can be used to present a problem in visual terms. This latter use is illustrated by a sequence from a mathematics lesson (B) (1966; secondary modern). The teacher wishes the pupils to realize that in using co-ordinates to describe the position of a dot on the blackboard it is necessary to establish conventional agreement that the horizontal co-ordinate precedes the vertical or vice versa. He could have used this principle without making it explicit, and left the pupils to follow; he could have 'explained' the reasons to them; he chose to represent the need to them in visual terms as a problem to be solved.

T   Now can you tell me what the position of the dot is in relation to those two lines? Glenys.

P   Two, eight.

T   Two, eight . . . what does it mean 'two, eight'? What does it mean? . . . All right . . . Sandra.

P Two squares up . . . eight squares across.
T Two squares up; eight squares across . . . rub that one out . . . and put another one . . . and what is this one?
P Six, three.
T Six, three.
P [another] Three, six.
T Just so; three, six.
P Three, six.
T Is it?
P Three, six.
T That is quite right . . . It could be three, six . . . Why shouldn't it be? What do you mean by three, six?
P Three squares from bottom; six squares across.
T Is he right? If he said three, six and asked me to mark a dot on this blackboard [makes another dot on the blackboard] . . . points one three . . . six . . .
Ps [untranscribable chorus]
T What must we do . . . to try to avoid confusion as to which of the two points is the right one? Can you, Janice?
P Count the bottom squares first and then the side squares.
T If everyone remembers these then there must be no doubt about it.

And there the teacher leaves the matter without making the principle any more explicit. It would probably have been useless to begin with general statements about the convention. Because they had grappled at first-hand with the problem of translation from a spatial to a symbolic representation, the pupils had experienced the ambiguity and therefore the need for the convention. (It could be argued that the teacher might usefully have asked the class to try to formulate a general statement; this cannot be decided here.) Moreover, this sequence avoided a fault already frequently illustrated in this paper, the fault of asking questions which fail to make explicit the criteria by which the answer will be judged. 'It could be three, six . . . Why shouldn't it be?' The child answering has to account for an ambiguity present to all the class; his responsibility is to this ambiguity, and not to unstated criteria guiding the teacher. This teacher has succeeded in objectifying his criteria in terms of the problem he has presented to the class.

The mathematics teacher of Lesson B had thus found a neat solution to the problem of making available to his pupils this part of his frame of reference. It is all too easy to let pupils know what to do without giving them access to the principles that would enable them to generate similar solutions in other contexts. If teachers wish their pupils to think rather than merely mimic, they need to find ways of making principles – the underlying rules on which their own thinking is based – available to the boys and girls they are teaching. In this case, this was done by making the problem available to the pupils in a non-verbal medium, but this is clearly not the only way of presenting them with evidence to manipulate. The nature of the problem was openly available: the children had grasped the need to communicate where the dot was and had shared the discovery of ambiguity. Language was not being used by the teacher for transmission: those pupils who answered questions were making explicit to themselves and their classmates the nature of an insight already partly intuited.

We can use this to throw light on some of the failures of communication in these lessons. In Lesson C the teacher interrupted her long description of Minoan civilization to ask:

T What kind of knowledge must the Ancient Minoans have had to build a palace like the palace of Crete and to be able to organize a whole drainage system and so on?

P They were very good at making things and building things.

T Yes ... Now, in order to build something you can't just gather the er building materials together and um start putting it up, you have to plan. What sort of planning ... what sort of knowledge do you need to be able to plan? Mary.

P You have to be an architect really.

T Yes ... Now, what kind of skill does an architect need? What kind of calculations does he have to make? He has to know what building material to use but also it's a question of how to use it.

P Do you have to have geometrical knowledge?

T He has to have a practical knowledge of maths doesn't he? [short omission] So there must have been architects living on Ancient Crete who had a practical grasp of the kind of maths needed to build a palace of this size and er magnificence.

At first glance we may assume that the question is too abstract for the class. They only reach the answer the teacher wants because she drops the clue 'calculations', and then it is – as far as we know – only one pupil who is able to use that. They are unable to answer the question because the teacher has failed to find a way of letting the class into her thinking. Complex buildings imply a whole range of practical skills and the knowhow that goes with them, but the pupils had no reason to select from this range the mathematical elements. The teacher achieved a kind of closure by dropping the clue 'calculations', but even the pupil whose answer was accepted ('Do you have to have geometrical knowledge?') shows by her uncertainty that she is barely following the teacher's line of thought, and certainly not adopting her frame of reference.

A similar failure to realize that for a child reality is organized upon a different set of matrices, so that the same words mean something different, is displayed in Lesson K (1967; history):

T Tell me about Homer . . . In what form did Homer write his stories?
P Attractive.
T Yes . . . it sounds nice . . . There's a sort of rhythm . . . a flow about it . . .

In this simpler example it is easy to isolate the word 'form' as the focus of misunderstanding, but could the matter be solved by a definition of 'form', as teachers sometimes seem to assume? In this case, the kind of knowledge which the teacher unconsciously assumes in his pupils would have necessitated more reading and writing of poetry and prose, *and discussion of their differences*, than is likely or perhaps possible by eleven years of age.

Let us now examine part of a biology lesson (E) (1966; grammar school) in which a teacher is trying to give a content to the terminology of her specialism.

T So the oxygen is taken to all parts of our body in the bloodstream. Now . . . how is it different in the insect? . . . Now, we did this in the last lesson . . . yes . . . ?
P Miss, it's got a lot of tubes in its body, Miss.
T The spider . . . er . . . insect has tubes running through its body. What are these tubes called?
P Trachea.

T Trachea ... Now, if an insect needs oxygen in a certain part of its body the oxygen goes direct to this part of the body in the trachea ... in these tubes ... so this is the difference ... it isn't transported or carried around the body in the bloodstream like ours is ... It goes direct to the party of the body that needs it using the tubes or trachea.

This well illustrates the difficulty facing any teacher who tries to use words to convey her systematic understanding of a physical process. What the teacher said in the previous lesson has become, 'It's got a lot of tubes in its body.' The teacher first makes a paraphrase into 'the insect has tubes running through its body'. She then (very skilfully) makes explicit the function of the trachea by contrast with human processes. It is possible that the pupil if questioned would have remembered some of this. But it would not be clear whether the teacher's language *meant to him* the structure and sequence which it meant to her. He might say the words, and yet still mean 'a lot of tubes'. It will only be through some reference from language towards what it represents – or towards some more direct means of representation, such as pictures or microscope slides – that the teacher will be able to ensure that her pupils are utilizing a frame of reference similar to that which organizes her own understanding of the process, that is, that they are *sharing her meaning as well as adopting her words*.

Some teachers behave as if they were confusing the teaching of language forms with teaching their meaning. In Lesson F the teacher is able to communicate with one boy through the language of his subject, chemistry:

P Please sir, could you purify the acetone to get it back?
T Well you can actually, yes ... by process of what?
P Distillation.
T By process of distillation ... We used it before ...

This grammar school pupil is unusual in his ability to think like a chemist and to use the specialist language. (It is worth noting, perhaps, that this sequence is unique amongst those we have quoted in that it is pupil initiated; perhaps the two characteristics are associated.) He and his teacher communicate easily. One of his companions is less successful.

(The teacher is trying to draw from the class the suggestion that acetone or carbon tetrachloride might be used to dissolve chlorophyll.)

T You've got the green stain on your trousers ... Could anyone suggest an alternative way ... other than by using water ... to get this green stain off again?

P Um ... you couldn't use shoe polish and then give them a good wash?

T No, I wouldn't try that [laughs] ... er I wouldn't try that on my new suit anyway ...

P Er ... er ... I mean floor polish.

T Floor polish?

P Yes, rub it in hard and then give them a good wash.

T Er when you've tried that way you'll have to let me know how it works [laughs].

The teacher failed to perceive what is patent in a transcription, that this pupil had reached the general idea of using a solvent. Since he had neither the general term 'solvent' nor knowlege of a specific solvent which would be appropriate, he cannot let the teacher know this. Therefore the teacher rejects what was potentially a highly relevant contribution.

In sharp contrast to this is a teacher who accepts a manifestly inadequate definition because it is clear that the child understands the word in its present context (Lesson B; 1966; secondary modern).

T I have written on the board this pair [i.e. the figures 7, 8] ... Will you mark the point ... which that pair ... denotes? What do I mean by 'denotes'?

P Where it is.

T Where it is. Yes.

This teacher is not so wedded to his term 'denotes' as to allow it to interpose between the child and the process he is learning.

It is the teacher of Lesson G (1966; physics; comprehensive school) who makes the most consistent effort to use language which will carry precise meaning to his pupils without building a wall of formality between them. 'The tin box only moves a tiny bit so the pointer has got to move a big lot,' and 'Why does the tin have crinkly edges?' and 'It would be really squashed-in-like.' Some teachers feel that this is a betrayal of standards, but this is probably not justifiable. Although the reader cannot tell whether 'crinkly' means 'serrated' or 'corrugated' or something else, this must have been clear enough in the lesson. Nor can the colloquial '–like' be objected to except upon grounds of social propriety. The language serves its purpose well: it directs the pupils' attention to the appropriate aspect of the apparatus, when the very unfamiliarity of technical terms might discourage attentiveness. If it is argued that pupils will later require a more specialized register at least for their written work, this may well be conceded. Yet this teacher, by encouraging pupils to talk about his subject matter in terms which they already possessed, was probably helping them more effectively towards this, than a teacher who threw his pupils in at the deep end of his own adult language. Because of an inadequate recording it is impossible to give any lengthy quotations of the kind of participation by the pupils which this teacher's informality made possible. Some impression of their contributions can, however, be gained from isolated questions such as: 'Please sir, if you go up a high mountain when you get near the top you can feel sick', and 'Sir, if you climbed a high height in a car, would the engine stop?' These are quite different from the contributions of any other class, even in the same school. It is easier to illustrate the teacher's style:

T This is almost the same as that one . . . a slightly different arrangement . . . cut in half . . . you see it? . . . little tin can . . . silver thing in the middle . . . silver thing with circles on it? . . . that's that tin can . . . tin can just like that one . . . all right . . . on a good day then what is going to happen to the shape of that? Is it going to go . . . down? . . . Do you know? . . . See what happens to the pointer. Well that pointer's got to be connected . . .

It seems reasonable to assume that this teacher's unusual language, informal and yet exactly adjusted to the apparatus, is related to his pupils' equally unusual degree of active participation in the lesson. This cannot have been merely the result of the teacher's linguistic style, but of what his speech itself implied, an interest in and attentiveness to the pupils' understandings and their attempts to extend them. Because he attended to their struggle to understand as well as to his goals as a teacher of physics, he was able to set up in his lessons an exchange of interpretations based on demonstrations with apparatus which boys and girls of quite limited ability were able to join in, and which even encouraged them to ask questions of their own. Such exchanges were sadly infrequent in the other lessons on which this paper was based, but it would be misleading to attribute this to the teacher's informal style alone. What we saw in this lesson was a teacher who presented apparatus which symbolized visually the principles he wanted his pupils to grasp, and who listened attentively to their attempts to think aloud about it. He showed that he took their contributions seriously, validating their efforts to understand by replying to them rather than evaluating them, as teachers frequently do in an attempt to control relevance. It seemed that it was his success in validating his pupils' thinking that made their participation in his lessons different from others, and encouraged them to initiate new issues and explore them aloud. Since it would be nearly five years before any of these pupils would have to demonstrate in an examination their ability to write formal scientific prose, he was surely right in placing his emphasis upon involving them in his thinking. Once a dialogue has been set up, the technical terms can be introduced in contexts which help the learners gradually to approximate their meanings to the teacher's, and eventually to adopt a style suited to writing about physics.

In revising this section it has been my intention to place only moderate emphasis upon the idea that the language forms that teachers use might be a barrier in their own right, though at times they may indeed import unnecessary problems into children's learning. It now seems more important to deal with them alongside other ways in which teachers present knowledge either as open to pupils' participation, open to discussion, interpretation, challenge and change; or closed, authoritative, and immutable. Technical language provides only one of the ways by which pupils can be deprived of the opportunity to discover that knowledge is a tool that can be used to understand and to change the world.

Teacher's Awareness of Language

This informal study was carried out with two groups of teachers acting as investigators. With both groups there was a marked change of attitude to the study when the analysis was made. Until that point the material had been in their eyes no more than recordings of ordinary lessons: the analysis, however, brought out implications which they had failed to perceive as observers of the lessons. And as they themselves were making the analysis, they did not resist these new perceptions, as they might have done had they been offered to them in lectures. Later they made further discoveries which had gone unnoticed in the first analysis: these came to light in group discussion. Thus, the study so far provides a basis for arguing (a) that some teachers fail to perceive the pedagogical implications of many of their own uses of language, and (b) that a descriptive study such as this provides a potential method of helping teachers to become more aware. Whether they are able to carry over this insight into their own work has not been shown, however.

Since these studies were carried out, many teachers have found it useful and enlightening to look at teaching and learning in a similar manner, often in their own classes. There now follows a list of issues that a group of teachers might choose to investigate informally, in order to increase their understanding of what goes on in their lessons:

(a) How does children's understanding of the world change and what part is played in this by talk? This might focus upon their concepts and how these change in discussion with one another and with the teacher.

(b) A second aspect of learning through talk: how can a teacher best set up a lesson to encourage valuable discussion? What are the virtues and weaknesses of small group discussion as against teacher-led discussion? What part might be played by 'evidence' – apparatus, maps, texts, etc.? How should tasks be defined in order to support and focus discussion? And so on.

(c) What roles should the teacher play in lessons? What encourages pupils to explore new ideas by thinking aloud and what discourages them?

Douglas Barnes

(d) If the central task of teaching is to make new conceptual schemes available to pupils, what part in this can be played by the technical terms which act as labels for those concepts? What is the influence also of the speech style that we have called 'the language of secondary education' and how can that best be introduced to pupils?

(e) Part of studying one's role as a teacher might be to look at questions as a partial indicator of the priorities that are being tacitly urged upon pupils. What patterns of questioning and replying encourage or discourage participation and thinking aloud?

(f) Another focus might be: how far does a teacher succeed in making available to pupils the underlying principles which structure what is being learnt? These principles often appear as the criteria upon which pupils' performances are accepted or rejected. If pupils do not grasp them, they can only fall back upon rote-learning or guessing.

The purposes of such study would be frankly pedagogical. Teachers would study examples of classroom interaction, and look through the language at the learning and teaching. The purposes would be quite other than those of theoretical linguistics as the subject is often taught in colleges and universities.

What is clear from this study – in so far as these teachers fairly represent their colleagues in other schools across the country – is that teachers would gain from a more sophisticated insight into the implications of their own use of language, and into the part that language can at best play in their pupils' learning. The present writer inclines to believe that, if such insights were made available to all secondary teachers, they would contribute dramatically to the effectiveness of teaching in secondary schools.

New Perspectives

Revising this report has made me aware of an overall change in the perspective from which I view classroom language. One way of putting it would be that I now know that my primary interest is not in language but in the learner's access to the means of learning. 'Access to the means of learning' does not mean merely the chance of speaking in classroom discussion. It includes the opportunity for exploratory talk and writing (for though this paper focuses on spoken language much of what I have said applies equally to written language) and it includes access to the principles upon which knowledge is based. One characteristic of good teaching is that instead of merely handing over approved knowledge or standard skills to pupils, it helps them to grasp underlying principles so that they themselves can see why the teacher judges this statement to be more valid than that statement, this way of doing things to be more appropriate than that. The importance of this understanding is that it equips them for a future in which there will be no teacher present to make judgements for them. During recent years some loud voices have been demanding that schools return to a supposed past when teachers taught subjects made up of authoritative truths. The present and future lives of students outside school will not however be made up of undeniable truths but of shifting, ill-defined and controversial possibilities: an education that does not help them to deal with this controversial world is shirking its responsibilities.

During the years that followed the first publication of *Language, the Learner and the School* I became engaged in studying the talk of children and adolescents working in small groups on tasks set them by their teachers.[13] This was only partly in order to extend the ideas put forward by James Britton in the paper that follows. Since I had pointed out that children in lessons are often prevented from advancing their understanding by putting thought into words it seemed necessary to demonstrate that they can in fact do so, and to illustrate some of the cognitive and social skills available even to children of modest ability. The prime purpose of the studies, however, was to show to teachers a range of ways in which pupils can be involved in describing, hypothesizing, suggesting, planning, criticizing, improving, solving and so on, if they could only devise classroom opportunities for them to do so, which is not always easy. It was not my purpose simply to recommend small group work, for that is no more than one option in the skilled teacher's repertoire.

Before moving on to summarize some of the outcomes of these studies, there is a useful distinction to be made between exploratory and presentational uses of language. When children discuss a topic without an authoritative adult their talk is typically *exploratory* – hesitant, often incomplete, hypothetical, directed not to making confident assertions but to exploring the range of possible accounts and explanations. The support of other members of the group seems to be crucial in this, especially the implicit support that comes from taking up one another's ideas and developing them. Exploratory talk seems to enact publicly the processes that Piaget called accommodation and assimilation, the bringing together of old knowledge and new experiences (or new ways of looking at experience) so that they modify one another. This is often to be contrasted with the *presentational* characteristics of children's responses to teachers' questions. Presentational talk is concerned with getting right answers, with satisfying a teacher's criteria, and not primarily with reordering the speaker's thoughts. It is likely to be abbreviated, and to focus more upon surface conformity to the teacher's requirements than upon understanding. Presentational talk serves the purposes of educational control, bringing pupils' statements into line with the teacher's frame of reference, and also offering the teacher the opportunity to monitor the effect of his or her teaching on the pupils' responses. Exploratory talk serves the purposes of understanding, giving the pupils an opportunity to reorder their pictures of the world in relation to new ideas and new experiences. The exploratory uses of language, both in speech and writing, are important because they lead to understanding rather than mimicry. When the learners have considerable control of the content and cognitive strategies, they are most likely to learn to think for themselves. Exploratory talk is infrequent in teacher-class discussion; only the physics teacher of Lesson G (see pp. 67–69) achieved it frequently in the lessons discussed here. Presentational talk is normal in lessons; the preceding pages show that although at times teachers succeeded in taking pupils through an important sequence of thinking, many question-and-answer sequences do not seem to engage with the learners' attempts to incorporate new ways of thinking into their action knowledge. Perhaps this explains why there are so few pupil-initiated sequences: the children do not perceive the presentational exchanges of lessons as opportunities for clarifying problems. When language is presentational the onus falls on the learner to produce an acceptable performance according to given criteria. This may often be appropriate. Yet we want young people also to be able to generate criteria of their own, and at times to criticize the criteria presented authoritatively to them.

During a later study of pupils' strategies in collaborative work on problems set by teachers, Frankie Todd and I were able to illustrate that under encouraging conditions thirteen-year-olds can engage in serious exploratory discussion.[14] We wished to show that adolescents possess abilities that are frequently untapped in lessons. These abilities include social skills as well as cognitive strategies. Amongst the latter, we found that boys and girls could (for example) set up hypotheses, modify one another's statements, advance evidence and arguments in support or opposition, and formulate new questions of their own. We were particularly interested in the occasional appearance of reflexive strategies: at best some of the thirteen-year-olds could step outside their own viewpoints, treating them as merely provisional, and search for over-arching principles in order to make sense of divergent views. Social skills seemed under these circumstances to contribute to their intellectual achievement, since the ability to collaborate, to qualify rather than reject, and to engage with another's point of view as an element in one's own thinking appeared to provide the necessary conditions for reflexive thought. It is not easy to illustrate these processes briefly; nor is thirteen-year-olds' language very like the language of secondary education, even though it can be seen to reach in that direction. The illustration that follows comes from a discussion about a question set by a physics teacher: 'Is work always done when energy changes form?' (The paraphrase is provided to help the reader to look beyond the informal style of the talk to the logical process of the argument.)

48	Marianne	Is, is there any things that we don't use energy in?	Marianne seeks an example to test an earlier assertion by Barbara.
49	David	Yeah.	
50	Marianne	What?	

74

51 David	Erm, one of these, one of pylons, holding up a roof, they aren't using energy.	Puts forward a relevant example.
52 Jonathan	It's constant energy, 'cos if that wasn't there the roof'd fall.	Jonathan does not use the given test for the change of energy from one form to another, but appears to be using a concept equivalent to 'potential energy'.
53 David	No, it in't moving is it? So it can't be using any energy.	David, using the definition of 'work', challenges Jonathan's assertions.
54 Jonathan	Well it had to use energy in the first place to be put up though.	Changes his statement to a form which acknowledges the validity of the test.
55 Marianne	Well it's using work.	Not (apparently) using the given definition of 'work'.
56 David	Oh to be put up yeah, but when it's there now, it just holds the roof up. It in't moving; it doesn't have energy.	David summarizes, relating to one another the two versions of energy previously put forward; he lacks a term such as 'potential energy' for labelling one of them.
57 Jonathan	There's a force, as well though.	Checking their agreement on the distinction between 'force' and 'energy'.
58 David	I know there'll be loads of force but there won't be any energy.	As above.
59 Jonathan	Uhm, no moving energy.	Jonathan is able to summarize because he has now fully assimilated the definition of energy via work.
60 David	There won't be any energy doing even ...	Incomplete

75

61 Jonathan	There's no energy transferred from one to t'other is there?	Now begins to move on to a further concept, accepting what has gone before.

It should be emphasized that these are not exceptional young people: they were chosen from pupils in a comprehensive school because their scores on an intelligence test were near to average. In this passage we see four of them applying their existing understanding to the set problem and, through a serious engagement with each other's accounts, clarifying for one another and for themselves some concepts their physics teacher had presented to them in an earlier lesson. Such clarification is not a mere intellectual luxury: if it does not take place – either in discussion or tacitly – the pupils would not 'understand' in any serious sense what they had been taught. Although this line of thought provides an argument for group problem solving as an item in the teacher's repertoire of classroom activities, it is at least as important to realize that it also sets up a template that can be used for evaluating teacher-led discussion. Does teacher–class talk provide opportunities for exploratory clarification and – more generally – for the development of similar social and cognitive strategies?

Another step in the argument was to consider *why* teachers adopt the teaching methods we had observed. It seemed probable, for example, that their expectations about the role talking and writing could play in learning were associated with their preconceptions about knowledge. This was important because it showed that teaching styles and the role assigned to pupils in lessons were not fortuitous results of 'personality' but were related to other aspects of teachers' roles. Some teachers seemed to view speech and writing merely as neutral means by which they transmitted information and checked whether pupils had received it: putting knowledge into words was not perceived to change the way in which it was possessed by the knower. Other teachers appeared to share my view that putting ideas into words played a central role in forwarding understanding. I tested these hypotheses by asking several hundred secondary-school teachers about the written tasks which they set to pupils.[15] Their replies were analysed with the help of a colleague, and shown to be distributed along a dimension which we called Transmission–Interpretation. This is how it was later summarized:

A teacher whose answers fell mainly or entirely in Transmission categories saw the purpose of writing primarily as the acquisition or recording of information. When he set written work, he thought mainly of the product – the kind of writing which he hoped his pupils would do – and of whether the task he set was appropriate and clear to the pupils. He saw marking primarily in terms of assessment, and either handed back written work to pupils with no follow up or used it as a basis for the correction of errors.

A teacher whose answers fell mainly or entirely in Interpretation categories saw the purpose of writing either in terms of cognitive development or more generally as aiding the writer's personal development. When he set written work, he was concerned with pupils' attitudes to the task being attempted, and was aware of aspects of the context in which the writing was done, such as the audience to be addressed, the range of choices available and the availability of resources. He saw marking primarily in terms of making replies and comments, and was concerned to publish his pupils' work by various means, and to use it as the basis of his future teaching.[16]

Why should these differences occur? It seemed that teachers saw the functions of writing differently according to whether their attention was primarily focused upon transmitting a body of authoritative knowledge or whether they were more concerned with the learner's struggle to make sense of the world. That is, certain views of the nature of knowledge seem to be associated with corresponding views of the role of language in learning. (This probably applies to spoken as well as written language but the transfer has to be made with care: some science teachers, for example, have told me that they take a Transmission view of writing but an Interpretation view of classroom discussion.) For an Interpretation teacher, written work gives the learner an opportunity to work on the problems he or she has in making sense of what has been taught, an opportunity to bring the new ideas to bear upon existing ways of understanding. The emphasis falls upon writing as communication between teacher and taught, encouraging the learner to engage actively with the issues raised by new learning. For a Transmission teacher, however, what is important is a body of authoritative knowledge with its associated values and criteria: the pupils' writing is either a record of part of this authoritative knowledge or an opportunity to test the pupils' performance against the ideal criteria. The emphasis in Transmission teaching falls upon acceptable performance; the emphasis in Interpretation teaching falls upon the learners' struggle to understand.

This can be used to reinterpret some of the lessons discussed in this report. The predominance of closed, factual questions, the exclusion of the pupils' experience and rejection of their struggling attempts to join in the teacher's thinking, the excessive use of technical terms and the failure to make principles explicit can now be seen as expression of a Transmission view of teaching and learning. Where, on the other hand, we found attempts to make principles available, to encourage pupils to put into words their attempts to understand, we had teachers who were (perhaps unknowingly) adopting an Interpretation approach. Although teachers of scientific subjects and foreign languages tend to come at the Transmission end of the scale, and teachers of English and religious education at the Interpretation end, with history and geography teachers between, it is nevertheless possible to find Transmission teachers of English and Interpretation teachers of physics. (When the same questions were given to teachers in primary schools their replies did not cluster in the same patterns; a different set of questions would be needed to elicit their preconceptions about language and learning. It would be interesting to find out whether there is a primary school equivalent of the Transmission teacher, whose attention is focused more upon the surface performance of reading, writing, number work and so on, than upon the processes by which children come to understand and make these their own.)

Related to these different views of the place of knowledge in school learning is a distinction that can be made between school and action knowledge.[17] It seems probable that we do not hold what we know in one undifferentiated system, but organize it in clusters of meanings around the activities or situations to which it appears to be relevant. It is a commonplace among teachers who teach two subjects, for example, that a class may not 'know' in a physics lesson what it earlier seemed to 'know' in a maths lesson; the clusters of knowledge tend to isolate themselves. 'School' knowledge is known in lessons, and is useful for answering teachers' questions, but never gets outside the school door to influence the 'action' knowledge by which a child organizes his or her daily life. I am not referring to different kinds of knowledge but to how any kind of knowledge is held by the knower. For example, someone may study animal diets in biology but not associate the information with feeding a pet until the two are brought together during discussion. Much school knowledge is quickly forgotten precisely because it is never integrated into the picture of reality which guides our actions. Transmission teaching, because of its emphasis upon ideal performance, is likely to maintain the barrier between school and action knowledge; Interpretation teaching, because it encourages the learner's attempts at understanding, tends to break it down. During the years since the original classroom study it has become clearer to me that I was uneasy about teaching that excluded the learners from taking an active part, not merely because it made it harder for them to learn but also because some pupils learnt at the same time that 'real knowledge' was esoteric and distant from the everyday things that they already understood.

At the same time as I was working with colleagues on Transmission–Interpretation and on the studies of small groups, other investigators – many of them sociologists adopting an interactionist perspective – were looking closely at classrooms.[18] Although they were frequently pursuing concerns different from mine, their studies often threw light upon relevant issues. Some I have already referred to in the course of discussing the lessons. Another was Sara Delamont; I should like to abstract from her work one short incident that throws a clear light upon differing conceptions of knowledge.[19] The incident occurred during a fifth-year biology lesson in a secondary school. The teacher was setting up the familiar demonstration in which part of the leaves of a plant are covered with metal foil in order to exclude light. After some days the covered and uncovered parts of the leaves are tested for starch to illustrate the function of sunlight in photosynthesis. One pupil, Michelle, was unconvinced and said: 'I don't see how that will prove it. It could be all sorts of other things we don't know anything about.' (She was right, of course.) Before the teacher could reply, another pupil, Sharon, broke in with: 'Of course it'll prove it. We wouldn't be wasting time doing the experiment if it didn't.' Delamont calls these two perspectives 'hot' and 'cold' science. Michelle wanted school science to be genuine intellectual inquiry. Sharon accepted cold science, an authoritative presentation of accredited knowledge, valid for examination purposes in exchange for certification. Transmission teaching encourages cold science; the pursuit of hot science requires teachers to adopt an Interpretation approach. Sharon was satisfied with 'school knowledge' but Michelle wanted 'action knowledge'. Schools offer not only cold science, but cold history, cold geography, cold mathematics and cold English. In many of the lessons we recorded in 1966 and 1967 it was cold knowledge that was on offer. The closed-ended and pseudo-questions, the religious education teacher who wanted the word 'pitcher' (p. 34), the geography teacher who omitted to mention she was seeing sand dunes from above (p. 42), the chemistry teacher who could not spare time for his pupils' attempts to join in his thinking (p. 28), all of these are the bearers of cold knowledge. These are the teaching methods that discourage pupils from thinking by rewarding unreflective regurgitation, by failing to make underlying principles available to learners, or by persuading them that school knowledge is inflexible, authoritative and the property of experts. In writing this, I am not pointing to teachers' original sin. The teachers were probably hard-working, competent and devoted to their pupils' interests. If we are to understand why they interpret those interests in the way they do, we have to look beyond the teachers as individuals to understand the context in which teaching takes place.

There appears to be a correspondence between teachers' views of knowledge and the teaching strategies they adopt in the classroom. This does not explain, however, why Transmission pedagogy and its accompanying 'cold' knowledge has such a powerful grip upon classrooms. The phenomenon is not a new one, though pressure upon teachers has recently increased. A survey of American research into teaching since 1860 showed a long tradition of 'guess what I'm thinking' questioning,[20] of the kind illustrated many times in this study, notably in the 'sand dunes' sequence (p. 42). The survey showed too that the various researchers who described this phenomenon almost unanimously condemned such methods because they provide a poor basis for learning. The study which my students and I carried out was unknowingly part of a long history of classroom studies which came to the conclusion that current teaching methods do not give the learner enough opportunity to organize his or her thoughts aloud. But why should this be? What survival value has Transmission teaching for those teachers who adopt it? One commentator has suggested that it satisfies the four primary concerns of teachers:[21] presenting a body of material, seeing that pupils achieve mastery of it, creating a positive attitude to the learning task, and managing the class. Yet this account itself seems to adopt a Transmission viewpoint by using phrases such as 'a body of material' and 'engendering mastery'. We are still left with the question: why do teachers so often accept and act upon such a view of teaching and learning?

There appear to be two kinds of answer to this question. First, a teacher faced with a classroom of unwilling learners may be forced back upon a Transmission strategy because a rapid series of questions is a ready way of holding attention even if no great learning results. To change from this strategy of overt control to an indirect one, in which the teacher manages the class by co-opting their interests, can be difficult. But to explain Transmission teaching solely in terms of immediate classroom problems is only a very partial explanation; to give a full answer we have to go out beyond the school and ask how schools relate to the rest of the society they are part of.

Teachers hear conflicting voices urging them to this and that. For simplicity's sake we will listen here to only two of them. One is the voice that urges the teacher to cover ground, to drill the basics, to prepare for examinations and to concentrate upon surface performance rather than upon the depth of understanding which is encouraged by voluntary involvement in learning. This first voice is a persuasive one, particularly now, when teachers know that their pupils will eventually have to go out into a harsh world of consumer riches and dwindling jobs. It is particularly persuasive because it often issues from the mouths of the pupils and their parents. The second voice has been more muffled of late. It says that schooling is not just for qualifications and employment, that at best it can offer the learner resources that are valid throughout life, not just in the competition for jobs. This voice urges that unless the learner's purposes become actively engaged, all that is learnt will remain school knowledge, to be quickly forgotten. Looking back after fifteen years I can see that my teacher-students and I were attending to the priorities of that second voice – though (if I remember rightly) both voices spoke from time to time in our discussions. Of course, teachers – especially those in secondary schools – have to listen to both voices and arrive at a compromise. In recent years, the first voice has become not merely urgent but hectoring, representing itself now as the voice of economic necessity, now as political policy, now as moral revival. It seems all the more important to listen to the quieter tones of the other voice, which insists that children are people too, that they are already making the choices that shape their personalities and lives, and that in a year or two they will have to take the responsibilities, social and moral, of adults. It reminds us of the possibility that if we treat them as if they were incapable of responsible choice we implicitly help them to be so. For me, the lessons we recorded in 1967 and 1968 were shocking, in the sense that I had not realized how far teaching could go in generating in eleven-year-olds an artificial dependency upon the teacher's fragile – and sometimes arbitrary – authority. It seemed a poor preparation for the adulthood so soon to come upon them.

I was once asked by a teacher whether I thought talking helped all learning or only some learning, and I am still trying to answer that question. Part of the answer must be that it is likely to aid any learning which goes beyond rote and which requires understanding. It is particularly important in those areas of the curriculum where reflective understanding of processes is important. But the teacher's question challenges me in a way which he perhaps did not intend. The knowledge taught in school can be either a tool or a straitjacket. By these metaphors I mean it can be either a means by which a boy or girl actively makes sense of the world or a source of mystification and discouragement. In discussing transcriptions of lessons all those years ago we were finding out (I believe) some of the ways in which teachers can make knowledge more likely to be a tool or more likely to be a straitjacket. It is probable that schooling prepares young people for adult life more by the processes they take part in than by the content they are taught. We cannot have too many citizens who have the habit and confidence of looking critically at those pictures of the world which are presented authoritatively to them, and who can decide what is likely to be true and what deserves their support. In a world in which many powerful bodies – including at times the State – wish to manipulate people's perception of themselves, their lives and their futures, citizens who found at school that knowledge is a tool and not a straitjacket will contribute to wise and just public policies.

What my students and I discussed in terms of effective teaching now seems to be related more profoundly to the cultural health of our society. When we thought we were talking about language we were also talking about making knowledge accessible; by showing, for example, that productive and critical thinking are not restricted to experts. Language forms now seem of secondary importance: specialist terminology and unfamiliar styles can be a barrier for some children, but I would no longer place a major emphasis there. 'Language' can also refer to the ways in which people communicate with one another, the roles the more powerful ascribe to the less powerful, the implicit according of validity to other people's remarks – or their rejection – in the course of conversation. Studying teachers' uses of language gives access to what I now see as the central issue, the allocation to pupils of an active role in what has been so happily named 'the conversation of mankind'.[22] This is not to pursue the chimera of a content-free autonomy for pupils. Mankind has in fact many conversations. Children's lives outside school provide them with a repertoire of ways of understanding the world; these need to be refined rather than rejected. And part of the business of schools is to offer access to other conversations that we call 'subjects' or 'disciplines', and to see to it that pupils become participants in those conversations, not mere listeners who parrot a phrase or two. This metaphor of learning as taking part in conversation should be put beside the other metaphor of knowledge as a tool rather than a straitjacket. The analysis of extracts from lessons which forms the main body of this report should be seen as exemplifying those two metaphors, making explicit distinctions between teaching that tends to involve learners in the conversation –

literally and figuratively – and that which does not; between teaching which offers the learner knowledge that can be used and that which presents knowledge as rigid, authoritative and intractable to the learner's purposes.

If we are to understand why teaching is as it is we have to consider the social, political and economic contexts of which schools are a part. It is not enough to consider only the espoused values of teachers or their immediate classroom concerns: events outside are likely to shift those values and redefine those concerns. During the last few years the education system has lost much of the public trust it once had. The economic anxieties of our time have been co-opted by some sections of the popular press, and by pressure groups such as the authors of the Black Papers, to persuade many members of the public that they want education to return to 'basics'.[23] In the terms I have used in this report, this means a return to Transmission methods of teaching, to 'cold' knowledge, and to requiring learners to accept a passive role. This has been accompanied in secondary schools by a change in pupils' attitudes to schooling. This is not merely a matter of 'the decline of deference'; much of the school curriculum is seen by pupils as irrelevant, whether it is or not. A substantial minority still accept school goals as leading to qualifications and perhaps to employment. Vocational courses are provided not only in colleges of further education but, with the encouragement of funding from the Manpower Services Commission, have moved downward into secondary schools. Vocational courses do not create jobs; their function must be different, to persuade those pupils who have rejected the academic curriculum that they are following a curriculum that will be of future use. Increasing unemployment will eventually challenge the credibility both of vocational and academic curricula. Particularly in city schools it has become increasingly difficult to persuade students that schooling makes sense. This is nothing to do with inefficiency or falling standards amongst teachers. Order in schools, like order in society, rests finally on cooperation, not on enforcement; disorder in secondary schools is a reflection of the collapse of credibility – in the curriculum and in employment. A return to basics will not recover pupils' confidence, whatever it symbolizes to their parents. Nor is an increased emphasis upon handwriting and punctuation, or even upon craft and technology, likely to create employment, develop new markets or improve productivity.

The education system is faced with a challenge. Will schools accept a role dominated by the functions of social control, selecting a minority of pupils for the traditional academic curriculum and contenting themselves with containment for the rest? Or will schools reject the demands for cold knowledge and Transmission methods and look for new curricula that can be shown to intersect with the world that young people are experiencing and will experience as they grow older? In helping them to understand and act upon that world the new curricula will (no doubt) now call upon traditional disciplines, now include elements of vocational concern, now look out at public issues, now turn towards personal experiences and goals. In *Language, the Learner and the School*, however, we have given first place not to the content of the curriculum but to the talking and writing by which teachers and pupils give it existence in classrooms. The best teaching has always strengthened the learner's own attempts to understand and participate in life, partly by validating and refining his or her existing ways of thinking, and partly by offering alternative 'tools' for understanding. At a time when education as we have known it is under severe threat, it is essential to reaffirm these values, and to show again what they can mean for that local but important conversation that goes on in classrooms.

References

1. Austin, J. L. (1962), *How to do Things with Words*, Clarendon Press.
2. Bartholomew, J. (1974), 'Sustaining hierarchy through teaching and research' in Flude, M., and Ahier, J. (eds.), *Educability, Schools and Ideology*, Croom Helm.
3. The term 'recode' is used in this way by Bruner, J. S. (1966), *Toward a Theory of Instruction*, Belknap Press, Harvard.
4. Woods, P. (1977), 'Teaching for survival' in Woods, P., and Hammersley, M. (eds.), *School Experience: Explorations in the Sociology of Education*, Croom Helm.

5. The term 'focusing' is used in this sense by Walker, R., and Adelman, C. (1975), *A Guide to Classroom Observation*, Methuen.
6. Rosen, H. (1966), 'The problems of impersonal language', an unpublished paper circulated at the Dartmouth Anglo-American Seminar on the Teaching and Learning of English. See also: Rosen, H. (1967), 'The Language of Textbooks' in Cashdan, A., et al. (eds.) (1972), *Language in Education*, Routledge & Kegan Paul/Open University Press.
7. Olson, D. R. (1977), 'From utterance to text; the bias of language in speech and writing', *Harvard Educational Review*, 47:3, p. 259, August.
8. John Olson points out the paradox of science teachers who recognize the restrictive nature of such an emphasis on words divorced from meaning yet believe such teaching to be necessary, and quotes one of them: 'Pupils supplying labels – you don't really need to understand what it's all about ... You can do that and be successful at it, but have no idea what's going on. It's menial in that sense but it is essential.' Olson, J. (1981), 'Teacher influence in the classroom: a context for understanding curriculum translation', *Instructional Science*, vol. 10.
9. This is not to ignore the process – sometimes called 'nominalization' – by which a group that has shared a sequence of experiences comes to represent their common interpretation of those experiences by a single word. ('Photosynthesis' would be an apposite example from biological science.) Yet in the classroom such economy of expression is counter-productive if teachers expect their pupils to understand and use the word before they have achieved sufficient order in the relevant range of experience.
10. Joos, M. (1962), *The Five Clocks*, Mouton.
11. Bourdieu, P. (1966), 'The school as a conservative force: scholastic and cultural inequalities' in Eggleston, J. (ed.) (1974), *Contemporary Research in the Sociology of Education*, Methuen.
12. Edwards, A., and Furlong, V. (1978), *The Language of Teaching*, Heinemann.
13. Barnes, D. (1976), *From Communication to Curriculum*, Penguin Books.
14. Barnes, D., and Todd, F. (1977), *Communication and Learning in Small Groups*, Routledge & Kegan Paul.
15. Barnes, D., and Shemilt, D. (1974), 'Transmission and Interpretation' in *Educational Review* 26:3, June, and in Wade, B. (ed.) (1982), *Language Perspectives*, Heinemann.
16. Barnes, D. (1976), op. cit.
17. Barnes, D. (1976), op. cit.

18. See for example these collections of sociological studies of teaching: Woods, P., and Hammersley, M. (1977), op. cit.; Woods, P. (ed.) (1979), *Teacher Strategies*, Croom Helm; Eggleston, J. (ed.) (1979), *Teacher Decision Making in the Classroom*, Routledge & Kegan Paul.

19. Delamont, S. (1976), *Interaction in the Classroom*, Methuen.

20. Hoetker, J., and Ahlbrand, W. P. (1969), 'The persistence of the recitation', *American Educational Research Journal*, vol. 6, p. 163.

21. Westbury, I. (1972), 'Conventional classrooms, "open" classrooms, and the technology of teaching', *Journal of Curriculum Studies* 5:2, November 1973.

22. The reference is to the title of Michael Oakeshott's monograph *The Voice of Poetry in the Conversation of Mankind*.

23. Centre for Contemporary Cultural Studies (1981), *Unpopular Education*, Hutchinson.

Acknowledgements

I should like to take this opportunity to acknowledge indebtedness that I failed to record in earlier editions. It was James Britton, Harold Rosen, Nancy Martin and other members of the London Association for the Teaching of English who first made me aware of the issues that this paper deals with, and my debt to them is great. I should like to mention too the encouragement and interest of Tom Hollins, then Director of the University of Leeds Institute of Education where the studies were carried out as part of courses leading to advanced diplomas. I should also have acknowledged the advice I received at an early stage from John Pride, now of Victoria University, Wellington. As in the previous editions I should like to thank the head teachers and their colleagues who allowed us to invade their classrooms with tape recorders, and the ten teachers and lecturers who worked with me in transcribing and studying the lessons: Mr G. Collins, Miss H. Corlett, Miss J. Ede, Mr R. S. Ellis, Miss D. Fawthrop, Mr A. C. Fraser, Mr E. R. Jenkins, Mr D. R. O. Paige, Mr J. W. Saunders and Miss M. H. Taylor.

Part Two
Talking to Learn

James Britton

We teach and teach and they learn and learn: if they didn't, we wouldn't. But of course the relation between their learning and our teaching isn't by any means a constant one. From any given bit of teaching some learn more than others: we teach some lessons when everybody seems to learn something, and other lessons when nobody seems to learn anything – at all events, not anything of what we are 'teaching'. As the syllabus grows longer we teach more – but do they learn more? And if we get three lessons a week when we ought to have five, presumably we teach more to the minute than we would otherwise: but again, do they learn any quicker? How *do* we judge how much is being learnt, in any case?

It's easy enough to test simple rote learning of course (from nonsense syllables through Kim's Game to the Thirty-Nine Articles), but this goes no way towards satisfying our idea of what learning and teaching *are*. We want children, as a result of our teaching, to *understand*; to be wise as well as well-informed, able to solve fresh problems rather than have learnt the answers to old ones; indeed, not only able to answer questions but also able to ask them. Information as to how well they're getting on in this kind of learning – even if we could spend half our time devising and setting and marking tests – would be terribly hard to come by.

With considerations of this sort in mind, it seems useful to take time off to think about learning, look for examples of it in progress, forgetting teaching altogether for the moment. If the teacher could be more certain what learning looked like, in some at least of its many guises, he might find it easier to 'monitor' his own teaching.

Since learning doesn't take place to numbers, however, and will probably sometimes take place in a very disorderly fashion, it is impossible to set it out, marshalled and docketed like the exhibits in a museum. Glimpses of it are to be found, first, in what people say to each other.

The first example presents a group of five sixteen-year-old girls talking about their homes. They come from the leavers' class in a comprehensive school, and the discussion arose as part of work on the B.B.C. Schools Radio programme, 'Speak'. There is no adult present.★ The transcript cannot show all that was said because every now and then snatches of general – or dual or triple – talk break out, and perhaps only a word or two emerges. But it is as faithful as I can make it. Since such a conversation represents people acting upon each other, I have tried to keep the speakers clear in the record by giving each an identifying letter. Words in brackets are what emerges from general talk or else unidentified interruptions – though as we shall see the term 'interruption' does not do justice to the supportive tone that most of the interpolations carry. Speakers B and D are West Indian girls, the remainder – as their speech indicates on the tape itself – are Londoners.

A This is always happening in our house. (Really?) My dad brings home things and ... you know, my mum comes along and she says, Right, this is no good, we'll get rid of this, we'll get rid of that, what's this doing here, we don't need this ...

B No, and doesn't ask first ...

C Load of old junk ... throw it out!

A You can't blame her really ...

B Yes, I know, but they have some things that you might think are old junk as well ... that could be taking up space, you know ...

A Like old exercise books ...

C Yes, you wouldn't throw *those* away for anything ...

B I mean ... I put certain things down in one place where I know they are and suddenly my mother comes and she says, Come on, we haven't got room for that ... (Yes, ... or she says ...) and I say, Well, where *can* I put it? Or she throws it away and says, Oh! did you want it? [laughter]

★The 'starter' for the discussion was an extract from a short story, *Now I Lay Me*, by Ernest Hemingway. The girls followed the suggestion for talk in the teachers' notes on the passage. Part of their discussion was subsequently used in the broadcast programme called 'Parents'.

C Sorry, but it was cluttering up the room . . . you might as well have thrown it away . . . it's no good.

A It's always causing rows in our family . . . My brother says, Where's my cricket set?

D I think it happens in any family unit, actually.

B I think it's just thoughtlessness for the other person . . . they probably think because you're younger, what you do have to put away is not worthwhile but as they're older people . . . you know . . . they . . .

A Have you ever . . . you know . . . sort of . . . Mum's said to you, like, Could you help me clear up? So you say, Yes, O.K., and you put your brother's or sister's things away, and then they come up and say, Where's so and so? (Yeah . . . Yes) But then you think to yourself, Well, it's annoying to have . . . to have . . . to leave somebody's coat or something in the middle of the room . . . (Yes . . . Yes, I know . . .) Do you know what I mean?

B And when they do complain, you feel as if you haven't done your job, but then you say, Well, I did pack it away, didn't I? . . . You know . . . what are they complaining about?

D It's annoying as well . . .

E I do the same . . . I mean if I find anything lying around . . . if it's no good I just throw it away . . .

A It might mean a lot . . .

D I think in my family . . . I think my mother is the most considerate . . . she'd ask rather than my father . . . my father wouldn't.

A Well, I'm lucky . . . I've got a room of my own . . . so . . .

D I'd like a room of my own, but then again, you don't keep everything in your room, do you? My dad or mother goes in there and finds anything that she doesn't think is necessary . . . my mother would ask me first, but my dad . . .

B Well, frankly, my mother wouldn't touch anything in my room, you know . . . she just doesn't. She feels I've put it there for some purpose . . . but again, if I go into her bedroom . . . (Yeah . . . That annoys me . . .) But say if I have a day off from school . . . or when . . . or we've got some sort of holiday and I see things around and I say, well, you know, I'll give the place a good old clean, at least it'll help . . . and I put things neatly, it's all tidy . . . I wouldn't throw anything out, because I'm not sure whether she wants it or not . . . and then she comes home, and she says, Where's this? where's that? . . . I feel awful . . .

D And you feel that . . . um . . . she doesn't appreciate . . .

B . . . appreciate, you know . . . I even the other day moved her bedroom . . . er . . . (Furniture) . . . furniture around.

D I did that in my house . . .

B I did . . . I thought it looked awful where it was, you know.

A But I . . . what annoys me is my room . . . is my room . . . If . . . if it's in a muddle I know where everything is . . . I like my room to be in a mess.

B But you see, we . . . I keep that as a sort of main bedroom, you know . . . (main room . . .) Yes, sometimes I don't even sleep in my room, it's so cold . . .

C Ooh, crumbs!

B How do you feel on this subject, Pamela?

D [with a great guffaw] Negative!

C I always know where everything is in my room even if it is untidy, but my mother comes along and I can't find anything anywhere.

A I like it when you get to that age when your parents seem to realize that you're . . . you're going off on your own . . . (Yes . . . You're growing up . . .) . . . you've got your own life to lead, so you think, Right, we'll leave all her things, she can do what she likes with them. It's her time, she can do what she likes with her time.

B They start from a certain point, don't they?

E Well, I don't think they always do that . . . They try to remember that you're growing up and then they forget.

D Yes . . . they try to protect you . . .

E They're treating you like children and telling you where to put things . . .

C . . . going round tidying up after you.

E You know, I usually arrange my bedroom as I want it and then my mum comes along. Oh, you'll catch a draught there . . . it's no good, you don't want it that way . . . (Yes. Yes.) . . . and they move it around you know.

A I feel like the bed by the window, but they say no . . . I like to look out you know . . . see what's going on.

B I like it as well, you know . . . I like the head of my bed to be right by the window, you know, and my mother comes along and she says, Where's the North Pole? you know, Where's north? . . . all this business . . . What's north got to do with it, you know . . . north and south . . . you know, you should have your head facing such-and-such . . . Oo, I think it's just fuss, fuss . . . I don't like it at all.

D They're trying to do their best to protect us but sometimes they do overdo it.

B And things like if I don't draw my curtains when I go to bed ... well, I like to see a half light streaming in, you know.

Already, it seems, the reader will be asking questions. How much of this talk is simply 'for the record' – an effect of the presence of the microphone? Does any individual girl in fact represent ideas that she really subscribes to? Or is each of them merely offering common currency, the small change of talk among their elders? Alternatively, in a different image, are they doing more than taking a nice warm dip together in comfortable beliefs that they all hold, have all talked about often enough before? Is anything happening to anybody in this talk – is anybody changing, or laying herself open to change?

Before pursuing these questions, let us look at a very different example of talk. A class of third-year girls (in their second year of Latin) was set the task of translating English sentences into Latin. They worked in groups of three, and here is a brief record of one trio:

A [reading] 'All the pupils are not praised by the teacher.'
B Where is it? [laughter]
C All the pupils are not ... third ... (Yes) Are ...
B Are not praised ... ([several voices] No.)
C Are not being praised ...
A Er ... to praise ...
C Um ... *antur.*
A So it's ...
B Yes, so its ... um ... *laudantur.* [writing] *Laud-ant-ur.*
A All right. So we've got that out of the way.
B We've got to make sure whether it's singular or plural ...
A Mm. They are ...
B They ...
A Yes, so it's right. Um ... now the subject (Pupils) ... which is er ...
B *Discipulus.*
C *Discipuli* ...
B *Discipuli,* yes, because it's plural.
C All the ... all the ...
B All the – what's 'all'?
C Mm ... don't know, is there a word for it?
A Yes, *cuncti.*
C So it'll be *cuncti discipuli.*

B Or *omnis* ... which shall we use?

A *Cuncti.*

C *Cuncti discipuli.*

B Mm ... by the teachers ...

A By the teachers ... so it's ablative ... So it's ... Yes, so it's *magis* ... [laughter]

C Um ... *magi* ... um ...

A You ought to know that.

C Yes, I know – ablative ... *Magistra.*

B I've got ...

A Now what does it read?

B *Cuncti discipuli magistra non laudantur* ... *laudantur.* [laughter] Yes – they are!

C Oh! you've got to have ... that ... shouldn't you?

B Oh ... um ... *A magistra.*

A Why?

C Yes ... *A magistra,* I think.

B *Cuncti discipuli a magistra laudabantur* ...

A *Laudantur* ... [reading] 'Heavy burdens will not ... will be carried by the sad slaves.' ... Heavy.

B *Gravis.*

C *Gravis.*

A *Onerus.*

C It's a passive verb.

B I know, but you've got the subject is 'heavy burdens' ... no, slaves are the subject, so slaves would be ... er ... *servis* Sad ... *tristis* ... *tris* ... *tristes.*

A *Tristis* ... *tristes* ... *tristes* ...

B *Servis* ...

C Um ... accusative, isn't it?

A No, it's ablative. Sad ... The verb will be 'will be carried'.

C The subject is ...

B *Portatur* ...

A *Portabuntur* ... Will be carried by the sad slaves ...

B *A servis* ... *servi* ...

C No, you should ... um ... heavy burdens is the subject, because that's what it's having done to it, you see.

B I know, but couldn't we ...

C Burdens is having the thing done to it.

A Yes, so you should start with the subject.

C Which is heavy burdens.

A *Onerus ... onera ... grava ... gravia.* Um – by the sad slaves, for the last
   time ...

The contrast between the two examples is evident enough, but they
are not offered in order that one should be accepted and the other
rejected. Their differences are of concern, but what is more important
is first to consider each as an example of talking to solve problems,
talking to learn. The problems facing the third-form girls were highly
specific: should it be *laudatur* or *laudantur*, for example. They were able
to commit themselves quickly, and their solutions, like the lights in a
crossword puzzle, would before very long be proved right or wrong.
To reach such solutions, however, they had to operate general principles, a kind of modified code based on the generative laws of the
Latin language. Thus behind the problem of *laudantur* lay that of using
the passive in Latin.

To a beginner, one might say, the use of the passive in Latin has
many pitfalls: and in any situation full of pitfalls, three watchdogs are
better than one. To that interpretation of the situation, however, at least
three things must be added. First, the girl least adept at manipulating the
passive in Latin is likely to learn to do it better by working with those
more adept. Secondly, even the girl who is most adept at handling the
passive in Latin is likely to improve her understanding of the principles
involved under challenge of being asked to *explain* what so far she has
accepted as 'obvious' or 'inevitable'. (As teachers we are familiar with
that form of the wisdom of babes and sucklings that consists in asking
the 'too simple' question.) And thirdly, one can conceive of a situation
in which the application of general principles presented a novel
difficulty that none of the group could solve at first, but which they
solved jointly by talking their way through it.

But what is to be said about the first example – the talk about rooms
and families by the sixteen-year-olds? Clearly they commit themselves
to nothing that can readily be proved right or wrong. They are not
arguing: no one seems particularly concerned to prove anybody else
wrong nor is anyone put in the position of having to prove herself
right. And as for the speed of the operation, the dominant impression

from the extract must be that if anything happens at all it will achieve itself in its own good time. If we ask, are the speakers merely supporting each other in already accepted familiar opinions (whether genuinely held or assumed, and whether prejudices or well-grounded opinions), we shall probably find it impossible to arrive at a satisfactory answer for the very reason already given – that the pace is leisurely and we need to see it cover a longer span.

That is therefore what I propose to do. But first something may be said on the basis of the extract already quoted. It seems fair to comment that the speakers do appear to be speaking their own minds: the consensus appears to be a consensus of their own views, not very much affected by the knowledge that adults may later be listening to what they say. There is a mixture here: some of the statements are complaints against their parents, invidious comparisons – things they might voice to their parents in anger, or even in cold blood, but not in the genial cum tolerant cum affectionate cum condescending tones of this talk; others seem to pose an adult view – or perhaps, rather, move towards such a view, Again, there are some observations that are clearly made from their own experience and not that of their parents – as, for example, when the 'good girl', by tidying up for her mother, gets in wrong with her brothers and sisters. In fact, if one were to hazard a formulation of what is beginning to happen in this extract, it might be to say that the group is gently probing to see how far it can go towards reconciling a daughter's viewpoint with that of a parent.

One direct outcome of a few minutes' talk by the third formers was a sentence in Latin: the sixteen-year-olds have nothing remotely like it, have in fact here no practical outcome directing their efforts. What they achieve in the way of learning – if they achieve anything at all – will have to be measured against some other yardstick. Here then the tape continues – back among the bedrooms:

B And things like if I don't draw my curtains when I go to bed ... well, I like to see a half light streaming in you know.

D The thing is, with my bedroom, I haven't ... can't have a view really, 'cos it adjoins the bathroom, you see, and ...

B Oh, I know.

C I have to share mine with my sister.

B You share with your sister?

C Yeah.

E I've got my own now but it's rather small ...

A I think it's a shame though ...

C A box-room, wasn't it?

E More or less ... yes.

A I think it's a shame when you live in a flat or a small house and your parents want the best for you and they try to get you a room on your own. My mum often goes round saying, Oh, if I had a big house, I'd have a music room and a reading room ...

B Yeah, all different rooms.

A They really want the best for you, you know ... you're pleased at that ... but the trouble is they feel as though they've not done all they could. (Yeah).

B And you don't want them to feel that way, do you? (No) Because you know, you can only ...

E The thing I like, you know, is when you come in in the evenings and there's only one room, one main living-room to go to ... and you have to get on with everyone, so you talk and say what's happened to you during the day and ... you know ... it's good to get on ... (Yes. Mm).

A It's also nice to have somewhere to get away from all the time. (Yes ... Yes, I think so) Because ... I mean ... at this stage, parents can be very annoying ... and ruin you ... They've got different ideas. I mean ... you know ... you might ... they might say something, you can answer them back ... and to them, just to answer them is being cheeky or impudent. (Yes) They don't realize you're just ... because you're talking to them as if they were a friend ... how I think it should be ... (Yeah. Yeah) ... they don't remember that, and they ... sort of ... you know ... sort of think, You're my daughter and so ... you know ... (Yeah)

D ... especially if I wanted to start a discussion on anything ... music perhaps ... my father would say, Oh, that ... symphonies and so forth are rubbish ... I mean, go on as if he was telling me off ... I'm only trying to start a discussion ... about music, and that ...

B Just a general argument. I think the trouble is, they're so used to putting their point and making it ... Well, that's that and it's right ... that when they get somebody that comes along and puts a different point to them ... makes a different point to the matter ... it's different ... they can't understand it, you know.

A I think that's a good thing ...

B And with my mother . . .

E You do?

A Yes. To have a row is good . . . it gets it out of your system. (Yes. I think so.)

B To have a row is good, I think . . . Well, the trouble with me I never stop at one thing . . . I always want to prove I'm right.

E My parents bring up something else what happened a long time ago. (Yes . . . Yeah.)

D My father is always referring back . . . I remember when you were ever so little, you never used to talk to me like that . . . I said, I've grown up.

B You couldn't, could you? But then again, in this book, there's another point, isn't there . . . I think this is the point . . . that the child talks about praying and how many people it prays for . . . and then by the time it's finished, it's daylight you know. And then, near the end, it says, but then again there *are* only two people.

A Two main people . . .

B Two main people there, yeah. But then . . . so . . . I think this signifies that whatever might happen between you and your parents, no matter what . . . they are there . . . and it means something, you know, just that they're there, even.

E There are some people that'll go through things with you that are nice . . . you know . . . to do, but when it comes to you asking someone to do something that's not very nice . . . you know . . . you hate doing . . . (Yeah) . . . they're always there.

B Your parents, yeah.

E If you have a row with a friend that you like, you know . . . that you get on well with . . . there aren't many people you can talk about it to, 'cause usually you're in a circle of friends that you all know each other . . . but your parents are always there, you know.

A It's all right for some people . . . I mean, it's not too bad for me . . . but some people can't talk to their parents . . . and girls can't talk to them. (No) With normal people, you know . . . it's still this, a mother and child.

B Do you think it's because . . .

A It's the same as some teachers who still think that . . . you know . . . We're the teachers and we've got to teach you . . . you're just the children . . . You know, they can't talk to each other as if they were sort of . . . on the same level.

D I don't think there's so much of that in our school though.

B No there isn't . . . I don't think there is at all . . .

At this point they spend a minute or two talking about school, about the need to learn how to put your own views and the difficulties of doing so. I am reluctant to cut the tape because one of the points I want to illustrate is the slow evolution that is one of the forms learning may take – and the need to give the process time. The *circularity* of much of the discussion will be clear. It moves on, certainly, with little hesitation and very little back-tracking: probably the only clear example of back-tracking – or a blind alley – in the whole tape is the exchange on p. 94 where a consideration of some relationship between rooms and sleeping – put forward by B – is rejected by D's 'Negative!' But progress is a kind of spiral: thus A on p. 99 drops a hint when she says, 'but the trouble is they feel as though they've not done all they could.' B takes it up and appears to be on the point of offering an explanation, but E interrupts with a point compelling enough to shift the course of the conversation. And the question of guilt – and its infectiousness in the home – does not return for some time.

To return to the tape for another extract or two – for, unfortunately, the record is too long to be given in full: B has firmly steered the talk back from school and related matters to the problems of the family. They talk about having to look after grandparents, with obvious implications about their own parents growing old, and this leads on to a pretty unanimous vote of confidence:

E I think that's part of growing up ... that ... um ... to know what your parents have said to you all along ... well, it's true (... appreciate the fact ...)

B Well, it's true, I can appreciate them more. To experience it in life and find out that it's true ... you know ... 'cause that's the best way ... when you experience it.

D Yes, it's hard to believe it even though it is your parents telling you.

A You don't seem to believe your parents, do you, until it happens and then you can't believe it ...

B No ... until you find out ... till you find out for yourself.

E I think round about now, you know, you start to realize ... your parents do know much better than what you do.

B I mean, you might not admit it ... ten to one you don't! (No) [laughter]

They go on to elaborate this confidence in their parents' views, mainly in terms of views about boys and dating. Then A breaks into a new vein:

A When we used to live in ... in Kennington ... they used to walk ... we used to walk across the bridge ... you know, walk around London ... used to be ever so happy and I can remember my parents walking along hand in hand ... you know ... giggling [laughter] ... and there's me in between, you know, looking up ... and laughing our heads off we were ... and I can remember that clearly as anything. It's one of the first things I remembered ... you know, being very happy, just the three of us. Then the next thing I remember was me having to go away because my brother was born and he had pneumonia ... and he came along and it was horrible ... (Yes) [laughter] ... It split up the family ... you know what I mean ... I was really jealous.

E You were out of things ...

A Yeah, I really got left out ... and it's been a bit like that ever since. (I think that, like ... Well, not only that ...)

B I think parents begin to get out of touch with each other as husband and wife ... slightly, I should think ... I don't know ... it all depends what the couple's life is like ... er ... when they start having children. You see it takes so much of their time ... and it takes a certain place in their lives.

A The husband gets left out a lot, doesn't he? (Yeah ... has a hard ...) [laughter] ... No, you hear such a lot ... when perhaps ... when your dad come home in the evening and your mother will say, Just a minute I'm getting so and so's tea ... Can you wait a bit? ... you know, he's probably come home from work ... (Yeah)

B Or, I've got my ironing ... or, I've got to take the children to bed ... and what not.

A Yeah, I think that's when they get ...

D My dad comes home and sits down and says, Will somebody get my slippers? and nobody moves, you know ... Everyone's eating their dinner or staring at the television ... He feels very neglected I think ...

B Probably because he feels everything should be done to him, you know. (Yeah)

C He's the father ... they should do everything for him ...

D Probably been ...

B Head of the house ... as it were.

A ... extra special attention ... which I think is right, you know ... I hope I remember that when I get married.

D He's the one that goes out to work ... earns the money, as he says.

B But then again, you find some families who ... don't take this attitude. They feel that ... both should be the sort of ... head ... you know ... leader.

A's recollection of her infancy encourages other girls to contribute theirs, and they give rise to such matters as parents who like to go out and those who like to stay in, the difficulties mothers have in getting out while the children are small, parents' attempts to educate their children and so on. Then E, who has not yet contributed an early memory (and who has said nothing for a while) launches the group into the topic of our final extract:

E I think what you mainly remember is when ... sort of ... to your knowledge ... your ... the first time you see your mother and father having a row ... Not a fight, but a row. (Yes) You always think ... you always look at them to be ... you know ... you think, That's my mother and father ... they're always so happy, you know, and I'm happy with them ... but when you see them angry with each other ... that just spoils everything. Sort of ... you can't say, you know ... then when you get older, you think, what if they got divorced ... or had to separate ... (Yes. Oh dear)

D It's on your memory all the while, isn't it?

E You think which one would you choose, and you can't ... well, I can't ... I couldn't choose between my mother and father.

A They seem to be one ... they are one. (Yeah. They are) Parents, you don't think of them as two separate people.

D You don't split them up into mother and father ...

A It's when they have rows that you realize they're two separate people ... what could go wrong. (Yes)

D I don't want to take sides ... I hate taking sides ... because my mum will explain ... she gets quite angry and she'll explain to me and tell me what happened ... and then my dad will explain. But the stories may be different ... you know, the same sort of thing, but different ... but I can see one of them isn't quite right and I can't say which one of them it is. (No)

C Have you ever had them say ... whichever one it is ... say you're always on his side? (Yes)

E   I could never take sides, you know ... if my father is ... you know ...
    shouting at my mother, I'd say, Don't shout at my mum like that! ... and
    then my mother will start shouting at my dad and I'd say, Don't shout at
    my dad like that! ... You know, I could never choose.

D   I can't.

A   I can remember the first row we ever had. It was ... I think ... my brother
    and I were in the kitchen and my mum and dad were rowing and it was
    so bad ... I'd never seen a row like this before, and my mum just started
    crying her eyes out and my dad felt terribly guilty, he was dead silent.
    Then I started crying, my brother started crying ... it was hell for about
    half an hour, you know. We all split up, there was nothing of the family
    left. And then we all crept back in, giggling and saying, Oh, I am sorry,
    you know.

D   Yes, that's the best part ...

B   Well, frankly when my parents ... when they do have rows, you know, I
    ... er ... always saw both sides, because there was something in each ...
    one's explanation that ... that meant something. (Yes)

D   You know, because each one's explanation was different, wasn't it?

B   Yeah, and there was something right in each one ... So I just couldn't
    realize why on earth they did have the row in the first place, because you
    ... you both have perfectly good reasons but they just don't fit in.

D   Sometimes they don't realize how upsetting it can be to the child. The
    child sometimes doesn't want to show they're upset in front of the parents,
    do they?

B   Yeah.

C   Sometimes it's something silly and the child could see it's silly and
    wondering why they're rowing over it 'cause they wouldn't think of
    anyone rowing over it ... it's just silly.

A   Yes, it's funny isn't it, children don't row so much as adults.

D   Really? [laughter] My brother and I, we row.

C   My sister and I are terrible ...

D   I think that happens to all families, doesn't it, when they've got brothers
    and sisters ...

E   Yes, but now I think you get most rows because they're *over* you, you
    know. (Yes ... Terrible) And you think you're the object of this row ...
    and you think, Ooh!

B   You're always getting the blame for everything.

D   ... and you're not really ... can't stick up for yourself.

B This is why sometimes . . . sort of lose contact with each other . . . because
   you sort of come between them in a way . . . you know.

There it is then: the whole conversation lasted about thirty minutes,
and of that I have given you some seventeen minutes' worth, ex-
tracting first from the beginning and lastly from very near the
end.

The language remains 'expressive' throughout, in the sense that it is
relaxed, self-presenting, self-revealing, addressed to a few intimate
companions; in the sense that it moves easily from general comment
to narration of particular experiences and back again; and in the special
sense that in making comments the speakers do not aim at accurate,
explicit reference (as one might in an argument or in a sociological
report) and in relating experiences they do not aim at a polished
performance (as a raconteur or a novelist would). I make this sketchy
analysis here in the hope of returning to it later.

In their comments and their narration, the speakers offer their own
evaluations of the behaviour they talk about: on the whole their
individual evaluations agree with each other. Some differences come
to light (as when A feels that adults quarrel more than children) and
here it may well be that an individual will revise her evaluation —
and of course there may be modifications made also to unspoken
evaluations. But in general it is a sanctioning process that goes on:
each enjoys the valuable social satisfaction of finding her evaluations
sanctioned by her fellows.

I would want to call this in itself educative — a kind of learning,
though rarely recognized as such. Our knowledge of the world is
inextricably bound up with the way we *feel* about the world, about
people and things and events and ourselves. Our ways of feeling, taken
overall, show a persistent patterning which constitutes our value
system. It is our values that make us the sort of people we are, and it is
on this basis of shared values that we establish our most intimate
network of relationships with other people. To define learning as
coming to know something about the world that we did not know
before, while denying the term to a *change in the way we evaluate* some

experience is to make a false disjunction. We need to recognize, moreover, that the network of people related to us by shared values provides, at every stage of life, the primary context for our learning of both varieties – both coming to know and refining our value systems. The maintenance of the two forms in close association can alone explain how knowledge can be at one and the same time both *personal* and *social*.

We should notice here that for the adolescents who make up the secondary-school population, this network of peers, mutually supportive on the basis of shared values, will be the seed-bed of a 'counter-culture' wherever such comes into being. Dare we hope that the kind of teacher understandings this book has set out to promote might contribute towards harnessing the energy of such a movement for positive ends? Part of the answer will certainly lie in the teachers' attempts to make in-school learning more like out-of-school.

As the talk of these five girls rolls on, we see as it were elements of the family situation laid out for inspection. They are not precise elements like 'subject' and 'passive' and 'third person singular', which when properly inspected and handled may come together as a Latin sentence. But they are there: parents are provided with a history – seen as young couples, with no children, free to go out; and as people with a future, old and needing help from those who now need them; and as separate people with separate likes and dislikes, though they usually feature in our minds as one; and as human beings capable equally of wise control and rows over silly nothings. Laid out also are the bits of the family jigsaw itself: father, the one who goes out to work; mother, the one who tidies – and is perhaps equally 'the leader'; brothers and sisters; grandparents, the not-to-be-neglected. And the various ties that link the pieces in various ways together: love, happiness, protection, anger, guilt.

I am particularly interested in E's last contribution and will try now to explain why. Quarrelling had come into the conversation early on – but then simply as a good way of clearing the air: guilt had been hinted at, as has already been observed. E's behaviour might suggest – though nothing can be said for certain – the gestation of an idea. Silent for some minutes, she then produces, rather belatedly, her contribution to the 'I remember' series: and when it comes it breaks defences that none of the group has yet dared to breach – and goes the whole way. We see her recoiling from the guilt involved in choosing one parent to reject the other, and finally – forcing the conversation back to make her last point – confronting the guilt of being the cause of all the quarrelling. Doubtless she could not say so, yet she seems to know – with us – that, of all the emotions that bind a family together, feeling guilty about each other is the most treacherous. E, if I am right about her, would indicate that there is here more than the laying out of the elements of the problem: something is done with them. There is a spiral movement in all that 'circularity'.

In talk of this kind trivialities may break in at any moment (though it is never easy to be sure what is trivial in somebody else's concern): it does seem, however, that as this conversation moves on it grows in its power to penetrate a topic and resist the trivial distractions. At its most coherent points it takes on the appearance of a *group effort at understanding*, and these coherent passages are more frequent in the later phases than in the earlier. There will be other virtues in argument and the clash of opinions: the mutually supportive roles these speakers play make it possible for them, I believe, to exert a group effort at understanding – enable them, that is, to arrive at conclusions they could not have reached alone and without that support.

If this is learning, it might be argued, then learning must be a very common phenomenon. No one would wish to dispute that: what I would argue is that a mode of learning so frequently practised ought to make more of a contribution to learning in school than, by and large, it is able to do as we organize things at the moment. And if teachers in fact came to the conclusion that it was no concern of the school to foster a better understanding among members of the family, their attention should still be drawn to this talk as exemplifying a means of learning that could be useful in other areas.

The emphasis we have placed, here and elsewhere, on expressive talk and writing has led to a good deal of misunderstanding and misinterpretation. One critic believes that the outcome of such an emphasis will be to 'imprison children in their common-sense concepts' (Williams, 1977, p. 47). But it is our view that the objective or scientific concept can only be arrived at by the modification of existing, common-sense concepts, however naïve these may be.

We believe it is of the very nature of human learning that it proceeds by anticipation. From early infancy we learn to incorporate a sense of the future into our perceptions of the present (Vygotsky, 1978, p. 28). The efficiency of our data-processing, when compared with that of the animals nearest to us in the evolutionary scale, cannot be explained on any other basis than this: we *prepare ourselves* for perceiving, we anticipate in a way that they cannot. And what is true of percepts in the early stages is later true also of concepts: we tackle an intellectual problem forearmed with alternative possible solutions. In this way human learning represents growth from a centre, a continuing programme. Typically, it is whatever is part familiar and part novel that beckons us on at all stages from an infant who imitates its mother's gestures to the scientist whose research investigates the borderline between the known and the discoverable.

Clearly, then, a learner's common-sense concepts cannot be left behind while he or she moves forward to contemplate, *de novo*, the new and unfamiliar – some statement of the scientific concept or evidence as to its nature. Rather, learners must bring with them whatever they already know and believe and attempt to re-interpret that in the light of the evidence offered. Interpreting the new and re-interpreting the familiar are the two faces of one coin. It is the language of their own intimate musings, their inner reflections upon experience, that will serve both to bring their common-sense concepts to the point of engagement with the scientific concept, and to carry out the reconciliatory interpretation.

Expressive talk and writing are means therefore rather than ends. Any expressive formulation of some piece of knowledge about the world is a potentially useful approximation to a more impersonal, objective, 'public' statement. But that is not all we can say: we must then recognize that that impersonal, objective statement will be appropriated and understood only as each individual who meets it is able to translate it into the language of his own reflective processes. Knowledge, in Michael Polanyi's terms, 'is an activity which would be better described as a process of knowing' (Polanyi, 1969, p. 132).

'Engagement', then, is a process of knowing, a process in which meaning is negotiated by constructing a version of the unfamiliar from the raw material of the familiar. In the kind of conversation we have been considering, the talk is itself an enactment of that process of engagement.

I think the reader will agree that those five girls showed considerable skill in the art of expressive speech. If expressive speech is a means of learning, they have at their disposal a pretty effective instrument. But, of course, the skill is something they had to *learn* – a fact that may not readily be recognized since much of that learning may have taken place before they came to school. Families will vary in the degree to which expressive speech is encouraged in the home: anthropological studies in recent years have shown amazing differences in the speech habits fostered and maintained by families in different sub-cultural groups living in neighbouring areas of the same town (Shirley Bryce Heath, 1983). Moreover, our uses of speech are so intimately dependent upon their context of interpersonal relationships that modes of speech acquired in one social setting (e.g. the family) cannot be relied upon to operate in another – even so open a setting as a self-chosen group of classmates in a school. There can be no doubt, therefore, that the skill shown by these five girls owes a good deal to their experiences in school – that is to say, it is to some degree a reflection of school learning.

Perhaps I can best put over the point I am trying to make by comparing the performance of those girls with that of two others. They are also school leavers, from a different school; they are discussing the same sort of themes. In this case there is a teacher present and though she is not saying much, the girls address their remarks mainly to her. Notice how little they generalize – how in fact when they embark on a generalization they seem very quickly to be drawn into particulars – and are likely to stay there long enough for the general statement to be forgotten. Thus it is difficult for one generalization to be built upon another. We may certainly draw general inferences from their particulars, but the speakers themselves do so rarely, and then perhaps incompletely.

A N . . . now, my boy-friend Tom, you know . . . now, if I go home and talk to my dad about him like . . . if I'm in the shop and something happens . . . it's funny or . . . see, I walked in the shop and he was piling up some ba . . . little pears, see . . . and I walked in and I must have slammed the door . . . I didn't mean to . . . they all fell down, see, so he said, That's the third time I've done that . . . so I did it . . . so I stacked them all up you know . . . and they fell down when I did it, so we both done it . . . and we got it all up . . . and I went home to tell my dad, you know . . . My mum said . . . er . . . Oh, that's all we hear about is him, we don't hear about anything else. And I don't talk about him all that much . . . but that particular time it's . . . you know . . . it was really funny the way he did it, you know . . . they all fell down, sort of thing.

B I mean, it's only natural to talk about your boy-friend, init? You'd think your parents would be interested, wouldn't you? My dad . . . he says . . . er . . . he says to me, I don't care . . . you know, sort of think, like that you know . . . My mum's all interested, you know . . .

T It's hard though . . . isn't it . . . hard for parents to be int . . . sort of interested in the proper way in boy-friends and girl-friends . . . 'cause aren't they bound to feel a bit sort of jealous of you . . . because you're their babies – going off, you know, into the world.

A Mary's mum won't let her join a . . . what is it again?

B No, well . . . you see . . .

A A youth club, see . . . Now, we can . . . we were going to join . . . [laughter from B] . . . last Friday. Now I said to my mum last night, Mum, I'll be going out Friday with Mary . . . on Saturday. Where are you going? So I said, I'm going . . . um . . . to join a youth club . . . said, Where is it? I said . . . um . . . I think it's South Borough . . . isn't it?

B No . . .

A I said South Borough . . . I don't know where it was.

B It's Smith Street . . . it's only up the road . . .

A Oh, Smith Street . . . anyway, so I says . . . um . . . We're going to join it, you know, and she says . . . umm . . . Oh all right then, you know . . . and she don't, like . . .

B . . . interested . . .

A . . . kind of ask you, you know, like . . . now . . . um . . . Monday I usually go round Tom's to help him sometimes you know with the shop because I . . . he serves and I give the Green Shield stamps out . . . and . . . um . . . anyway she . . . um . . . I usually go in there Fri . . . Mondays and Sundays to help him sometimes . . . anyway I goes down there Friday, and I gets back at seven o'clock . . . that's when the shop shuts, and we went out.

Anyway, when I got back about nine o'clock I said to Tom, I'm going back now ... said I don't fancy ... I wasn't all ... I didn't feel all that ... good ... good, you know. Anyway, so I went home and I ... when I'm not feeling well I go all quiet, you know ...

B ... sulky ...

A Anyway, so I'm just sitting there watching telly ... she said, What's the matter? Now if I have a row with Mary we usually make it up the next day, didn't we?

B We come to school ... say something like, Hi-ya, girl!

A Yeah. But then ... um ... she say to me, Oh you had a row with so and so so and so, you know ... and she'll keep on and on at me, you know, till I do ...

B 'Stead of trying to cheer you up, sort of thing ...

A Yeah, she'll keep on and on so in the end I just walked out. I just went out for a walk, you know ... I thought, can't I keep something to myself? You know ... the things I don't want to tell her I don't, you know ... I don't go home and tell her things that ... er ... I want to do like an ordinary child does ... I keep them to myself ... or tell my dad ...

B I do that sometimes ... Do you think parents ... like they all make out if you sit indoors, you know ... nothing to do ... and they always saying, Why don't you go out, you know, or do something, you know, and when you find something to do like join a youth club or go a pictures with your mates ... they won't let you go ... it's silly, don't you think, though ...

T Well, I suppose parents get into just as much muddle as children do, in a way.

One of the inferences that might be drawn is that made by some of the teachers from that school: they believed that to help the girls to 'get somewhere' in their talk was one of the most generally helpful things they could do for them – something that would assist their work in all parts of the curriculum.

What does help mean in this case? First, of course, it means providing opportunity and an atmosphere of confidence and encouragement: that this was being done is clear from the tape. Secondly, it means entering into the talk at the right moment and in the right way. A tentative generalization offered opportunely in the give and take of conversation is obviously more helpful than any string of generalizations could be, spoken to a silent class. Such a contribution or, at a later stage, the question that invited the speaker herself to generalize – these would be life-lines to cling to when the whirlpool of particularities threatened to suck her down!

The struggle to organize their thoughts and feelings, to come up with words that would shape an understanding – the struggle to rise above the limitations of their language – can be sharply felt at times when reading the record:

B You know why that is . . . 'cause . . . 'cause when . . . when my brother and I was young you know, like, he used to hit us ever such a lot, you know . . . but when we . . . 'Cause he used to hit us so much my mum threatened to go to the police one day, you know . . . and ever since that day he's never touched us, you know . . . and I think . . . and he never used to show us any attention . . . you know, when your mum and dad sit down and sort of read to you and try to teach you things . . . and all things lke that, you know . . . and sums and that . . . he wouldn't do nothing like that . . . and my mum used to say to him that he won't get on with them when they get older if you don't take no attention to them . . . and he never took no attention to us at all . . . and I suppose that's why, init really? . . . and it just won't work out now 'cause he's left it too late, hasn't he? you know what I mean?

A final comment – though not one to be too serious about: at the end of this conversation they had come up with no better solution to their problems than the one they started with – a solution as particular as it was impractical:

A . . .my dad should marry her mum . . . and your dad should marry my mum and . . .
B . . . we both go and live with our mum and her dad, and let our other mum and dad get on together . . .

On the morning after they had finished taking their C.S.E. examinations, four boys were talking to their English teacher – and part of the conversation is the next example. She asks them what they thought of their fifth year at school: one boy (B in the transcript) states his views: 'I mean, like, if you can get the same job the year before – the same job as what you're going for if you stay on at school a year there's not much point in staying on, is there?' The teacher asks, 'Then what do you think education is for – to get you jobs?' And so the topic of education is taken up. It rapidly turns into argument. A thinks you have to be educated 'so that you can go out and take over from the older generation that are getting old and take on civilization and put it forward, like'. His argument is based, mainly, on the necessity of *invention*. C is in favour of education 'so that you know what you're on about'. (Someone refers to him as a motor-bike addict, and he is certainly knowledgeable about cars.) B declares his respect for education because it 'makes you a better citizen', but apart from indicating that being educated saves you from taking up crime he does not say what he means by being a good citizen. Being mad on cars he has picked up a great deal of know-how with regard to them – by watching and having a go – and he values this sort of knowledge, which seems to him to have nothing to do with education. D sides with B on the whole, and particularly opposes A on the grounds that the ability to invent things comes from experience and not from education.

The teacher is occasionally drawn into the ding-dong, but more often comes in as a kind of chairman – trying to get a sharper definition ('Well, what do you mean by that?'), or to untangle particular knots ('Yes, well, what's the other counter to C's argument?'), or to broaden the perspective ('You're still seeing it in terms of jobs'), or occasionally to sum up the position reached.

The conversation lasted about forty minutes: what follows is a record of the last six minutes or so:

T This education you're talking about you know ... it's just the acquiring of skills. Don't you see education as doing anything else?

A Educating.

T I mean what about all the other subjects? Supposing ...

B It broadens your mind ...

T Supposing somebody was an absolutely superb mechanic ...

B Yes?

C Yes?

T I don't know how you would assess that somebody was superb as a mechanic ... but there was absolutely nothing that defeated him, and he could turn his mechanical skill to any vehicle – in fact any kind of machine

... One would have to admit that he was in that respect an educated
man ...

C No, you wouldn't.

T You wouldn't? Oh! I see ...

C You wouldn't have to admit that he was educated, it's just that he's ...
gone into a job as an apprentice ...

D He's just a craftsman.

C ...and he's gone up in his job until he's top mechanic. He knows what he's
doing. Same as you in your job. You know what you're doing, didn't you?
Half the time!

D He's a craftsman, ain't he?

C As my ...

A But he had to learn it. He just didn't get it like that.

B Listen, listen ... He says you've got to be educated to come out and learn
a job, right? Learn a trade, right?

A You can't go out right dim?

B All right then, listen ...

C My dad's a dumkopf – but he knows what he's on about.

B My dad came out of school. He left at fourteen, right?

A Yes.

B He went in the print. He jacked that in 'cos he didn't know nothing, he
wasn't educated ... he admits it ... but then he went into an apprenticeship
for plastering. Six years apprenticeship, right? Now he left school at
fourteen.

A Yes ... so he's six years ... he had to learn about it first ...

B I know, but you don't have to be educated to learn about it.

A I know – in special subjects you don't.

B You say you've got to be educated to do things though.

A You have got to be educated to do some things.

C Look, my dad can't tell mutton from ... my dad, he's as dumb as me when
it comes to maths. In fact he's dumber than me – he's dumber than me at
English. Yet look at the job he's got. He's working in the print. He's
worked as a barber. He rides motor-bikes, right? He used to do that as a
job. He used to be a chauffeur. Now you can't tell me that to go out and
get on a motor-bike and ride it and to drive a car, you've got to be educated.

D Eh – so you've got to be educated. Now listen to this. My old man, right?
... he hardly went to school from about he was twelve, right? Because he
was evacuated in the war, right? And he started off as a job, you know
like, as a welder. He started off as a welder and then he went into lorry-

driving, right? Long distance. Now he's a manager. Where'd he get the education from that?

A   Yes, but you say, look, when these people invented these things ... they weren't ... they weren't ... they weren't as ... like us, were they? ... years ago ... They weren't like us. They were rich people mainly ... who'd been to school because their people ... their parents had sent them to school ... who invented all these things?

B   People ...

A   And they were educated.

C   They had to pay to go to school.

A   And during the war, people who invented things had been to school.

B   People during the war ...

D   No, it wasn't ...

A   Near enough all ...

D   People then ... to do experiments ...

B   No ... 'cause all they had is the roof over their heads ... which wasn't too safe.

C   We're not talking about during the war ... we're talking about the first aeroplanes and cars and that ... The blokes that invented them ... in those days when they were invented ... to go to school your mother and father had to pay enormous sums of money ...

B   Not necessarily ...

C   ... and most of them went to school.

B   And what happened if you went to orphans' school?

A   And that proves your point that you've got to be educated.

B   No, it doesn't though ...

C   Yes.

A   None of us people, right low down in the working class ... they never invented hardly anything, did they? It was rich people – because they'd been to school.

D   So they went to school – so they went to school. They're not going to learn about engines and that because they hadn't been invented ... They invented them when they left school.

A   That's what I mean, and ... yes, they was educated, wasn't they?

D   What for? They hadn't got to be educated about engines.

C   They had to work out the compression ratios, gear ratios, everything like that. You can't do that without maths, can you?

B   A one ... a one-cylinder engine ... the compression ratio is slightly easier to work out.

C Yes, but a little kid of four couldn't do it, could he?
B I know . . . he hasn't got the mental ability.
C No – neither have I. I couldn't work out the compression ratio.
B You haven't got the mental ability of a kid of four . . .
C I know . . . well, then . . .
B You couldn't . . .
C You can laugh . . .

The argument is good tempered in a bantering way, but gets quite heated as it goes on, and makes a fairly noisy tape. The sharp retort, the flat contradiction, rejection both by counter-statement and by abuse, a steam-rollering use of repetition, and occasional fierce competition to be heard – all these features set up a very different situation from the mutually supportive talk in our first example. Above all the speakers set up what is tantamount to a demand on each other to be *more explicit* – and the teacher does so deliberately. To comply would require a move from expressive speech to a more *referential* mode, from speech that tells us a good deal about the speaker – his feelings about teachers, about the topic under discussion and about his particular, current contribution to it – to speech that designates more accurately, refers more specifically.

Look however at the following exchange taken from this argument:

B As I've said before . . .
C 'It makes you a better citizen!'
B Well it does.
T Well, what do you mean by that?
B Well, if you've been educated you appreciate things more, don't you? Right . . . so if you see someone's nice new shiny car, you won't go up with a dirty great knife and go crr . . . crr . . . down the side.

C's mocking quotation of what B has said several times before might suggest that in C's opinion they don't get much further by merely repeating that formula: he doesn't say so, but rejects B's contribution by a mild form of abuse. The teacher does ask B to explain, to be more explicit. His reply, 'you appreciate things more', is clearly not more but less explicit – since one who appreciates things more might presumably make a better lover, a better husband, a better artist, a better tenant – as well as a better citizen. However, B's example then indicates that it was a better citizen he had in mind – if we accept his assumption that appreciating cars more is what makes you respect another man's property. In exemplifying what he means he is in a sense being explicit, but only in a sense: it is not the *idea* of 'being a better citizen' that is made explicit, only the example – the idea, the generalization, is implicit in the example, not explicit.

It does seem that these four boys are linguistically more advanced than the two girls in the preceding example: in response to the demands of the topic, and of the activity they are engaged in (argument), they do produce a considerable number of general statements. Yet repeatedly, at just the point when a more explicit generalization is demanded, they respond with a particular statement, some kind of exemplification. When, for example, A makes his claim that you need to be educated 'so that you can go out and take over from the older generation . . . and take on civilization and put it forward', he gives, as examples of people having done this, the invention of aeroplanes and 'getting to the moon'. He is then taken up by B *at the level of the examples*: 'Anyone can make aeroplanes that have got the plans and all that in front of him.' It is by a series of similar steps – interactions at the level of example – that the argument finally breaks down in the long extract printed here.

In the course of the discussion as a whole, quite a few of the ideas needed to explain what education is and what it does are referred to. For example:

'That's instinct, isn't it? That's just curiosity – what you were born with.' (A)
'When we get older like, we discover about things about us.' (D)
'mental ability' . . . (B)
'been brought up that way . . .' (A)
'apprenticeship . . .' (B)
'you need experience . . . if you worked by 'em and worked with 'em you could . . .' [build an aeroplane] (D)
'you have to learn by doing it yourself' . . . (C)
'You'd stand there and you'd watch and you'd learn. That's education – learning.' (A) 'No, no – you learn yourself.' (D)

Some of the useful elements of the topic are thus 'laid out'. But, in the heat of the argument, very little is done with them and certainly they are not manifestly put together to arrive at any solution, any resolution of the conflicting opinions.

There is also, as might be expected, a wealth of exemplification: Boeing 707s, space flight, the teacher's car, primitive tribes, cave-men, the Mafia, munitions workers – all these and many other things are brought in to serve the speakers' arguments. They fail to do so, as we have seen. To realize what view of education is implied by another speaker's example means envisaging *alternative possibilities* to the view you hold yourself: and these boys seem able to do this only fleetingly and partially. They make very general statements on the one hand and give concrete particulars on the other: the one is too general to provide a testable hypothesis and the other so particular as to constitute in itself no hypothesis at all. The intermediate generalizations needed to bridge the gap are something they can neither supply for their own statements nor derive from other people's.

I have quoted B's early remark: 'I mean, like, if you can get the same job the year before . . . there's not much point in staying on, is there?' To a varying extent all the speakers make use of such expressions as, 'I mean', 'like', 'sort of', 'you know' and the question tag after a statement – 'is there?', 'would he?', 'don't you?' and so on; and they all at some time use the term 'right' in a somewhat similar fashion. Expressions of this kind have been called (by Professor Basil Bernstein) expressions of 'sympathetic circularity'. They constitute an appeal to the opinions and sentiments held in common by the group. 'I mean', 'like', 'sort of' and 'you know' seem to operate sometimes as indicators of a break in the process of putting one's thoughts into words – a break which the listener is invited to fill in for himself from the shared stock of unformulated opinions: at other times they seem to appeal for confirmation of what follows. The question tag is an appeal for confirmation of what has just been said – confirmation, again, from the shared unspoken resources.

There are plenty of these expressions of sympathetic circularity in the mutually supportive speech of the previous examples – the five girls and the two. One might hazard a guess that such signals would feature in speech of that kind, but disappear when speakers engaged in argument. Bernstein has, however, suggested the contrary: that when speakers of what he calls 'a restricted code' – a form of language which tends to be associated with the expression of shared attitudes and opinions rather than of individual differences – when such speakers are put in a situation requiring the elaboration of *differences*, they will tend to use the question tags all the more as a means of reducing 'sociological strain' – the anxiety, perhaps, they feel when they seem to be losing the support of group solidarity. It was interesting to note in the transcript that, as the argument warms up, 'like', 'sort of', 'I mean', 'you know', 'don't you?', and so on, tend to be replaced by the more emphatic form of appeal, 'right[?]' (which is sometimes a question – a demand for agreement, and sometimes a statement, a claim that there is agreement). If we divide the conversation into three equal parts, 'right[?]' occurs seven times in the first third, once in the second, and fourteen times in the last third, while the comparable figures for the other forms are thirty-six, thirty and sixteen.

I had a growing feeling as I studied the transcript that each of the speakers had some difficulty in believing the others could *seriously* hold an opinion different from his own. They appear to become puzzled, even aggrieved, as differences develop. At one point B makes a statement, C contradicts him and B says: 'No, no mucking about now, because, I mean . . .' and a little later C interrupts him with, 'No, come on . . .' At all events it seems that each speaker supports his case by an appeal to something the group already accepts and possesses rather than to something they could now work out for themselves: that is to say, an appeal to *common sense* rather than an appeal to *reason*. The two are very different: common sense, it seems to me, is not a system of logically related, rationally held ideas; it is rather the accumulated representation of what one has 'got by with' in the past – an amalgam of factual knowledge, loosely empirical evidence, intuition, untested belief. If the appeal to what one takes to be a commonly held 'common sense' fails, and the appeal to reason cannot be made, the end is likely to be – as in this example – exasperation.

Argument seems to have a limited value for boys and girls whose powers of talk are at the stages of those we have been considering. Even at a later stage, a good argument may put us on our mettle, but it is likely to be the thinking we do *after* it that is productive rather than the thinking we do in the heat of the dispute. The mutually supportive joint exploration, using a great deal of expressive language, is likely to be more productive *at the time*. I have suggested that A's contribution in the first example may illustrate the gestation of an idea: I suspect that a leap-frogging of listening and speaking may in fact be the characteristic feature of a joint exploration in talk and account for its value: each may give what he could not have given had it not been for the 'taking', and in turn what he gives may provide somebody else's starting point. If it works that way, talk would indeed be a cooperative effort yielding a communal harvest.

But clearly there must be the opportunity also to explore differences: it cannot be true that people can discuss usefully only matters on which they think alike. I wish to make two observations here. First, teachers need to find – somewhere in a larger context – an area of agreement within which their pupils can discuss differences. Failing that, they are space walking and that doesn't get them anywhere. It will follow that there must be some matters that cannot profitably be discussed between some people. Second, I want to refer to a form of discussion described by the American psychologist, Carl Rogers, and christened, therefore, 'Rogerian debate'. Roughly described, this is a process in which A tries on B's viewpoint and sees how the world looks from that angle – in particular that bit of the world about which differences of opinion have arisen. B is there to assist him and 'check his position'; when he is satisfied that his view has been adequately stated by A, he listens while A tries to say what he *finds in common* between his own and B's points of view.

A last word on the argument: we need to bear in mind the possibility that a satisfactory understanding may be reached, in ways that we do not yet understand, by the handling of implicit rather than explicit meanings. The difference between the two might be roughly similar to the difference between common sense and reason – though probably it would be more accurate to think of it as the two kinds of understanding which, in adulterated form, enter into 'common sense', and in purer form might be called reason on the one hand and intuition, imaginative wisdom – even poetic wisdom – on the other. Some of our group felt that the lack of explicit generalization and appeal to reason in the argument on education was not as crippling in its effects as I have represented it to be. Certainly, the joint exploration in expressive talk, and some informal modification of 'Rogerian debate', might prove valuable ways of handling implicit meanings; as well as a way of moving from the implicit towards the explicit, from expressive towards more referential uses of language.

The last transcript in this section differs from the others in many respects. The occasion is a science lesson with a first-year secondary school class, and the talk arises out of what the boys are doing and have been doing – heating copper in a flame. Again, though a good deal of talking went on among small groups of boys during the lesson, what is recorded consists in the main of what the teacher says. He talks first to small groups and later to the whole class. The tape comes from a film made by the Nuffield Science Project. (It was not possible to distinguish all the boys who speak, but A, B, C, etc., have been used to differentiate as far as possible the members of the group taking part at any one time.)

T Right, now. What do you think?

A It went . . .

B It's turned silver.

T Turned silver? Are you sure it's silver? Take it up to the front and have a look at it.

A It seems to have gone . . . red.

B . . . green.

T Yes, it looks as though it changes colour. What happens if you scrape it? Have a look.

B It's going . . .

A It goes pink . . .

T Do you think that's something that's formed on the outside, or what?

A . . . think it's . . . er . . . formed . . . er . . .

T What's happening then?

A A film's forming . . .

T A film? You think this is coming out . . . coming from inside the copper, do you?

A Yes.

B ... combined with something in the air ... to form the film.

T So you think something in the copper is ... doing what?

B Is coming out ... well, is combining with the air and forms that film.

T Yes. And what do *you* think?

C The same.

T You think the same? Well, *what* do you think – you tell me then ... since you say you think the same.

C I think ... there's something that's ... er ... combining with the air ...

T Something combining with the air? Do you think you could think up an experiment to see whether the air is important in this?

a Yes ... well ... we could ...

T Yes, well you think about it. I'm going to ask you all in a minute when you line up round the bench. All right?

A Right.

T O.K.

T Well, what about it then, A ...?

A Well, sir, it got ... with something in the copper.

T Well where do you think it's coming from, this black powder?

A From the flame.

T From the flame? ... something coming out of the flame? ... See if you can think up something ... You think it's coming out of the flame. Do *you* think it's coming out of the flame?

B I think it's coming out of the copper, sir.

T You think it's coming out of the copper? Well, B ... see if you can think of things you could do ... another experiment which would show which of you's correct. Anyway, think about it and I'm going to have you all up at the bench in a moment.

T [to the class gathered round the bench] Right, then. We've got three theories as to why the copper turns black when it's heated. We've got A's theory, which has six supporters, saying that it's something coming out of the air. We've got C's theory with four supporters saying that it's something coming out of the flame. We've got F's theory with eighteen supporters saying it's something coming out of the copper. Now obviously you can't *all* be right – and you've had some time to think over and work out an experiment to help verify your theory. O.K., then, A, what's your experiment?

A Well ... suppose that's ... air, I guess ... It would be a good idea ... um

... to ... um ... put ... a piece of copper foil in a ... in a ... in a tube and ... and put a cork in the end, and then take the air out of it with a vacuum pump. And then heat it ... If it turned black again it would prove our idea was wrong, but if ... if ... if it doesn't change, our ... it would be right.

T Do you agree with that, B?

B Yes.

T Good. Now, what do the flame people think? [no answer] What do you think, C?

C Use another sort of foil and if that turned black then you'd know it was something in the flame. If it didn't, it wouldn't be something in the flame.

T Yes ... any idea what particular foil?

C Lead foil?

T All right, we might try that. What about D, you got any ideas?

D No ... the same one, sir – use aluminium.

T All right, well we'll try it ... But can anyone think of a way by which they could heat the copper so that the flame won't actually come in contact with it? What could you do to ... E, any ideas from this group?

E Sir, you could ... er ... put copper foil in a test-tube over the flame ... then the flame won't be getting at the copper.

T Good – that's a good idea, isn't it? If you heat ... if you heat the copper in something where the flame's not actually touching ... Now, F, you're the spokesman for the copper school. Now have you got any ideas on this?

F Well, you ... you could repeat ... um ... A's experiment, and if ... um ... if the copper turned black, that would prove us right ... um ... but if it turned ... if it stayed its norm ... it would prove A's group wrong as well.

It is a brief extract, but even so I believe it will speak for itself to most teachers. 'Alternative possibilities' are very much in the air – indeed certain alternative possibilities are what the lesson is about. And because they are possible ways of explaining something pretty concrete and specific, and because differences in the explanations offered are going to be resolved in the end by further concrete happenings in the laboratory, one may miss the essential importance of the theoretical processes involved.

The first phase – the talk in small groups – is directly concerned with possible explanations. Though the teacher's questions are obviously a great help, he begins on each occasion with a very open question:

'What do you think?' and 'What about it then?' – saving his more directive questions until he finds they are needed. No doubt they will be needed less as time goes on – and more will come from the boys in response to the open question: indeed, in response finally to events themselves, regardless of the teacher. I was struck by his questions to C in the first group: he seems to believe there is some virtue in having C formulate for himself rather than take over B's formulation. I believe also that the movement in words from what might *describe* a particular event to a generalization that might *explain* that event is a journey that each must be capable of taking for himself – *and that it is by means of taking it in speech that we learn to take it in thought.*

The second phase is the mustering of the alternative explanations and, from there, the devising of means to verify them. The ideal in this – the most difficult part of the task in hand – is that all the possible explanations of a proposed experiment should be taken into account. Are there some that would consider it a waste of time, therefore, that the teacher did not do this part of the job himself? He does in fact lay the burden on the boys' shoulders, and waits patiently while they talk their way through.

They are using in this extract – both teacher and pupils – a spare kind of language very different from that in most of the other examples. The reason for this lies in the nature of the activity of which the language forms a part. At the roots of scientific activity lie empirical operations: what is *done* in the chemical laboratory is of central importance and the language that serves such operations is closely related to processes – a language that may often be barely intelligible to someone who can't see what is being done. And when at the next stage (as in this example) words are used to explain the effects of what has been done or to devise plans for what *shall* be done, the generalizations must maintain firm connections with the concrete data. True enough, wild speculation has its place in scientific activity, but the process of applying it, harnessing it, is one of re-shaping it in appropriately *specific* forms.

The spare look this language has may mislead us into thinking that it can easily be learnt. But the task is not that of learning a language; rather it is that of acquiring, *by the agency of the language*, the ability to perform these mental operations I have been talking about. *A child's language is the means*: in process of meeting new demands – and being helped to meet them – his language takes on new forms that correspond to the new powers as he achieves them. Expressive speech is one of the more accessible forms; the language of scientific hypotheses, spare though it may appear, comes later.

I think at the time of writing this we believed that expressive talk would manifest itself in the classroom if we as teachers merely indicated our willingness to accept it. It seemed to us that the strictures normally set up for classroom discourse prevented its appearance, and once those strictures were removed, expressive talk, so familiar outside the classroom, would prevail also inside it. This certainly proved not to be the case. We learned from experience that expressive talk has to be *earned* rather than simply allowed in. That is to say, mutual trust between teacher and pupil has to be established before expressive talk can flourish, and mutual trust cannot be created in terms of speech behaviour alone. Appropriate speech behaviour on the teacher's part is a necessary but not sufficient condition; rather, teachers must prove to be 'as good as their word'. Martin Buber goes so far as to suggest that this relationship of mutual trust is the key to all that school education can achieve: trust in the teacher breeds trust in the world – trust on the part of the individual child in his own ability to make sense of the world (Buber, 1947, p. 98).

Much that is involved in this notion has yet to be explored: it has powerful implications for our conception of a teacher's authority, for our conception of curriculum, and for our understanding of the purposes of schooling in our society.

Taking a narrow, professional view of ourselves as teachers, we might claim that our authority lies in our expert knowledge of a particular field, our 'subject' on the timetable. In so many words, our successful achievements as a student of that subject conferred on us the right to teach it. Critics have not been slow to point out that this conception of expertise in institutionalized education in a literate society falls a good deal short of the non-institutional, pre-literate view by which the teaching was entrusted to a successful *practitioner*. Our confidence in ourselves as teachers is likely to be more vulnerable when we base our claim on *knowledge about* rather than on *role performance*. More materially, an authority derived from such expertise is effective only in so far as the student covets for himself the knowledge and skill we can teach him. This means that it is destined to meet failures in every classroom, and not least for the reason that the brand of expertise offered appears to the student to have little to do with any social role performance appropriate to his present or predictable life. Thus it is that management techniques, the policeman aspect of a teacher's job, come into play, for to maintain conditions in which learning can take place is an essential part of a teacher's responsibilities in school. It is at this point that we discover that being an authority on Jane Austen does not make us an authority over Tom, Dick or Jane.

In exercising this managerial authority we are the agents (in differing degrees on different occasions) of the corporate group that makes up the class, the social institution that constitutes the school, and the wider community in which the school operates. I have been fascinated by the way new teachers arrive at the discovery that the managerial role is both (a) necessary at times and (b) of no use in the actual process of teaching. Intuitively, they proceed to develop a teaching/learning relationship with each individual pupil, while maintaining a potentially managerial role *vis-à-vis* the group as a whole – exercising it less and less until it becomes no more than a potential role and the teaching/learning relationship has virtually taken over.

It seems to me that intuitive processes of this nature are essential in learning to become a teacher, and continue to be essential to good teaching. Yet so many of our approaches in teacher-education tend to discourage rather than encourage such processes. The conventional concept of 'the student who has earned the right to teach' puts far too much stress on what the teacher knows and directs attention away from what the students know, what they need to know, and the means by which they can be helped to know it. Living with this concept long enough, we as a profession tend to become bad learners, anxious to teach ourselves rather than trust our teachers (Hargreaves, 1982, p. 201), and bad listeners. The listening is in my view crucial: with all the pressures of class teaching it has to be fought for strenuously. If it is the students only who have to listen, they are denied a major part of the *action* that makes up *interaction*, and without interaction we regress to a discredited view of learning as a uni-directional process, proceeding from the teacher to the student. The distortions arising from this view lie behind a good deal that Douglas Barnes has criticized in the first section of this book. Take, for example, the way a process of 'guessing what is in teacher's mind' will often substitute for genuine discussion. Yet genuine discussion is *exploratory*, an opening out of possibilities in order to arrive at a configuration, a nexus of some kind; guessing what is in teacher's mind, on the contrary, is a closing-in process, a mental variety of 'hunt the thimble'.

A recognition that talking can be a means of learning; that its effectiveness as such a means relies on a relationship of mutual trust between those taking part in the talk; and that the onus for establishing that relationship in the classroom lies first with the teacher – all this clearly assumes an interactive view of learning; and this in turn has important implications for our view of curriculum.

An 'output' model of curriculum, one which sets out its description in terms of pre-planned outgoing behaviours to be achieved by those taking the course, is clearly consistent with a uni-directional view of teaching/learning: the stress is on what the teacher will do, and this is something he can determine and describe in advance. An interactive view of learning demands something much more flexible. What can be planned in advance is a set of teacher-provided resources which may or may not be called into service. The aim here is to conduct a course that makes sense to a student as he *looks back* over it: a teacher is able, from past experience, to make available resources likely to stimulate learning, even in unforeseen ways; that is to say a degree of planning of the *input* is possible. But the difference is not simply one of the predetermining of either output or input. There is a sharp difference in the amount of pre-planning that is possible, and in the flexible model consistent with an interactive view of learning, a process enters in that has no counterpart in the output model – the process of *negotiation*. Provision is thus made for unforeseen learning to take place, both because of the pre-planned resources, and because input is invited from other sources – from the students themselves and from the shared experiences of all concerned from one day to the next.

We may advocate such a programme in very simple terms – in terms of the advantages of learning with each other and from each other. Yet the processes involved are complex: not only is it true that such a learning programme makes sense to a student as he looks back on it; it is furthermore a *corporate* experience, treading the knife edge between satisfying individual needs and interests and maximizing the effect of shared experiences, common interests and social responsibilities.

A good hard look at curriculum by teachers who have learned from experience what student talk can achieve, what interactive learning means, how much students can contribute when curriculum is negotiated, what kinds of cooperative learning flourish as teachers become better listeners – I doubt if there ever was a time when this was more sorely needed than it is today. Where relationships of mutual trust make corporate learning experiences possible, I believe a model is provided and a mode of operating established which could enable school leavers, over a wide range of interests and abilities, to become responsibly independent learners for the rest of their lives; not learners for the sake of learning (or even for the sake of teaching), but learners from experience who plough back into responsible social behaviour the fruits of their individual learning. Such a belief should challenge us as teachers to resist those aspects of the hidden curriculum in our schools that work in a contrary direction, rationing knowledge, reducing perspectives and hostile to change.

There is no doubt that public policies for education are today far less supportive of the ideas we have outlined in this book than they were when it first appeared in 1969. We may, however, find encouragement in the fact that there has been since that time an increasing body of research findings consistent with these ideas and effective in extending our understanding of the mental processes involved. But perhaps we should be encouraged above all by the way sensitive and committed teachers continue, as others have done over the centuries, to find their own way – by honest intuition and a confidence in their own experience – to an interactive view of teaching and learning. I came across this piece of encouragement in my recent reading. Published in 1916, it is a third-person autobiographical account of events that took place in 1895; the writer is Dorothy Richardson –

un-trained governess turned un-trained teacher in a school in Finsbury Park, a north London suburb:

> She had discovered that the best plan was to stand side by side with the children in face of the things they had to learn, treating them as equals and fellow-adventurers, giving explanations when these were necessary, as if they were obvious and might have been discovered by the children themselves, never as if they were possessions of her own, to be imparted, never claiming a knowledge superior to their own. 'The business of the teacher is to make the children independent, to get them to think for themselves and that's much more important than whether they get to know the facts,' she would say irrelevantly to the Pernes [the three sisters who own and run the school] whenever the question of teaching came up. She bitterly resented their vision of children as malleable subordinates. And there were many moments when she seemed to be silently exchanging this determination of hers with her pupils. Good or bad, she knew it was the secret of her influence with them, and so long as she was faithful to it both she and they enjoyed their hours together. (Richardson, 1979, p. 333)

The examples of talk included in this section have principally been examples appropriate to work in English lessons. I think most English teachers would recognize the fact for several reasons: the topics discussed have largely been personal experiences, accounts of events that featured relationships with members of the family, with boy and girl friends; contributions to the talk very frequently took the form of narratives – experiences were reconstructed in order to share them; and contributors seemed more concerned to express how they felt about these experiences than to present a full and accurate record of events. While these three characteristics might not be the first things that come to mind when we think of literature, we should have to agree, I believe, that they are as relevant to and as true of literature as they are of the recorded conversations we have been considering. I suggest it is these common characteristics that make literature, on the one hand, and the shaping of experience in order to share it in anecdote, on the other, equally appropriate material for the curriculum of English lessons. It is no mere accident that the stories told from personal experience in the conversation of the five school leavers developed from a discussion of a piece of literature.

Talking to Learn

Work in English, as work in any of the arts, has as its principal objective the mind of learning we characterized as concerned with the way we *feel* about the world – that is to say with the generation and refinement of our value systems. I believe learning in all subjects of the curriculum involves both 'coming to know' and the adjustment of *values*; but that in the science-like subjects the former is dominant, whereas in the art-like subjects it is the latter that is dominant.

What is important is that the two modes of learning should complement each other and achieve a kind of balance. It is the purpose of this book as a whole to stress that both modes of learning rely upon specific uses of language and that the quality of learning in all subjects will improve when we as teachers apply a fuller understanding of the language-using and learning processes.

References

Buber, Martin, *Between Man and Man*, Routledge & Kegan Paul, 1947
Hargreaves, David H., *The Challenge for the Comprehensive School*, Routledge & Kegan Paul, 1982.
Heath, Shirley Brice, *Ways with Words*, Cambridge University Press, 1983
Polanyi, Michael, *Knowing and Being*, Routledge & Kegan Paul, 1969
Richardson, Dorothy, *Pilgrimage I*, Virago, 1979.
Vygotsky, L. S., *Mind in Society*, Harvard University Press, 1978.
Williams, Jeanette T., *Learning to Write, or Writing to Learn?* N. F. E. R. Publishing Company, 1977.

Acknowledgements

I should like to thank the following for help with transcripts and permission to quote from them; the British Broadcasting Corporation (page 92), Miss Margaret Frood, Mr John Kerry, Miss Nancy Martin, Mr Martin Richards, Mrs Pat Smyth, Miss Margaret Tucker, Unilever Ltd and the Nuffield Science Teaching Project (page 121) and Mrs Elizabeth Webster.

Part Three
Language Across the Curriculum: Policies and Practice

Mike Torbe

Language across the curriculum was a product of a time and a place. It was connected with political and cultural changes in the ways teachers were thinking and feeling about their students and about the purpose of schooling, at a time when everything seemed to be changing. Harold Rosen's 1971 description of the process reflects the optimistic enthusiasm of the days of discovery and experiment:

For many years we busied ourselves with our own fascinating specialist concerns with what did or would happen in the two hundred minutes per class of curriculum space allocated to us by the time-table. Increasingly, however, we found ourselves being pushed beyond the boundaries we had come to accept or perhaps helped to create. We found ourselves discussing the relationship between language and thought; how language represented experience; the functions of language in society; different kinds of language and how they were acquired; the difference between talking and writing; the nature of discussion and group dynamics. Inevitably we started to trespass in areas marked 'Keep Out', though some colleagues waved a welcome from the other side. There were others peering over fences, those engaged in integrated studies, group work, inquiry methods, environmental studies, social studies and innovations of all kinds. Some of them, though not many, were also concerned with questions of language. Soon we found ourselves talking about 'language in education', or 'language and learning', and finally about 'language across the curriculum'. We felt sure that language was a matter of concern for everybody, that if children were to make sense of their school experience, and in the process were to become confident users of language, then we needed to engage in a much closer scrutiny of the ways in which they encountered and used language throughout the school day. For this we needed all the help we could get from other subject teachers.

We started with talk. At that time an emphasis on talk did not seem to be a radical idea: the word 'oracy' was already being used by educationalists alongside 'literacy' and 'numeracy'. We soon discovered, however, that the unanimity was a superficial one. *The Schools Council Examinations Bulletin*

No. 11, for example, phrased the problem like this: '... they [the Steering Committee] recognize that the language of the coffee bar is not appropriate to school', and 'An idea of examiners deliberately coming down to the lowest teenage level was rejected, although the problem of contact was recognized' (p. 196).

By contrast, we were far from sure that we knew enough about the language of the coffee bar. We had certainly not settled what might be considered the appropriate language for school, though we knew quite well what was usually considered appropriate. It was largely for this reason that we began by looking closely at the language of children in various kinds of contexts and roles, both in the presence of adults and on their own. The questions we asked ourselves were:

What are the different kinds of talk used by children and young people?
What are their different functions?
How does the size and nature of the group affect the quality of the talk?
How do different kinds of talk develop in the school years?

We began making tapes of children talking in different situations. We discovered that what we believed to be reasonably skilled predictions – we are all experienced teachers – were in many cases very wide of the mark. We had imagined, for example, that a tape of children preparing a meal would show them engaged in discussion, and even argument and recrimination, about fair shares, about who does what and the organization of clearing away, about how much they should leave for the adults, and so on. Instead of which the eating of food was accompanied by talk addressed to no one in particular which simply named the foods, and the organization was carried out quietly with only one or two subdued reminders – more in the nature of spoken memoranda than exhortation. We discovered more too about the effect of the presence of teachers – the way, for instance, the presence of a respected and appreciated teacher created a sort of psychological and social space in which less assertive children could make a contribution and all members of the group could engage in sustained talk. And most important – since it is the kind of pupil activity that most teachers by definition do not see much of – we learnt to sketch in the outlines of the folklore of jokes, reminiscences and attitudes which held the group together when there were no adults present. (Normal children spend a great deal of their time laughing.) In this way we became more certain that smaller groups were essential for certain activities and that only small talking groups could address themselves to problems in the way that so many children on the tapes had done. Almost without noticing it, we began to talk about language with scarcely a thought of school subjects.

Our next move ... was not only to be concerned that the talk of school-children should be given new importance and attention, but also to subject all uses of language in school subjects to closer scrutiny. We had found ourselves concluding that if we were committed to the development of children's language in school, then we needed to take a practical step towards making some impact on the way in which language was used throughout all the processes of school learning. This in turn meant that in any given school there needed to be a common approach to the uses of language. This task was in one sense straightforward and in another bristling with difficulties. It was straightforward because we aimed at drawing up a brief document – a 'manifesto' was the first grandiose term we used – which set out in unadorned terms what we thought ought to be done. It was difficult because we wanted the 'manifesto' to present a view that was relevant to teachers of subjects other than English.

In those times of change, teachers increasingly recognized the individuality and value of children's lives and welcomed the cultures that children brought with them. Language across the curriculum was ideological: it endorsed openness and identity, valued the children's own experiences, and set out to dissolve boundaries, so that school and home were no longer in different worlds. It raised questions about authority, about who could make decisions, about the education of *all* children – mixed-ability teaching was an important element. It was, clearly, a radical political act to present that 'manifesto', as Harold Rosen called it.

Another main thread was not political but theoretical. Psychologists had been interested for some time in the development of young children and in the ways they learned. Piaget, Bruner, Kelly and, especially, Lev Vygotsky had presented theories of child development, intellectual development and learning which questioned traditional ideas about teaching. Their work explored the close relationship between thought, feeling and language, the way the human intellect operates and learns, and how it uses language to do so: indeed, there were strong hints that the way human beings learn their native language was a model of all learning. Once teachers began to ask how children learn their own language, the answers led them to inspect critically the whole process of teaching and learning in school.

The commonest theory of learning is modelled on the way a book works: it is about uniformity, continuity and lineality, to use McLuhan's formulation (McLuhan, 1974). Learning is seen as a logical and rational process, because 'rational' has for a long time also meant uniform, continuous and sequential. But 'logic', as Susanne Langer points out (Langer, 1942), is not a mode of thinking but a technique for evaluating or checking a thought. *Understanding*, which ought to be the purpose and the outcome of the educational process, entails simultaneity, a grasp of a field of knowledge and a perception of interconnections, and is likely to be reached not by following someone else's logical presentation but by creating one's own pathways. A part of the politics of language across the curriculum was an assertion of the right of an individual to learning.

That theory reaffirmed the rightness of paying close attention to children, and it underpins this book. The argument is as follows. Human beings learn by constructing a 'model' of the world in the head, by creating, in Kelly's words (Kelly, 1963), 'working hypotheses which are about to be put to the test of experience'; and that 'world representation' is constantly revised, adapted and extended by being matched against the flux of new or familiar experiences around us. Although that process does not only operate through language, language is its most explicit and most fully articulated expression. The relationship, then, between, thought and language, though obscure, is close. What at first happens openly in speech, at a later stage of growth and development seems to happen internally as thought (Vygotsky, 1962); but we never wholly abandon the inner speech which is one manifestation of thought. There are processes of inward storytelling, of telling ourselves, of talking silently to an imaginary interlocutor, which are as much part of 'thinking' as operating abstractions and pushing around concepts. There are leaps of imagination involved in all learning which seem to be non-verbal; on the whole, however, it seems that not only does thinking generate speech and writing, but that speaking and writing themselves generate thoughts and learning.

We learn by using language, by talking and by writing; learning is an act of creation which makes and shapes the world of the learner. Learning is not the passive acceptance of other people's ideas and pre-existing knowledge, but is an activity undertaken by the learner. If that is true, then in school learning both students and teachers must use language actively. The students' meeting with new and difficult information, and their turning it into personal knowledge, must be active as they test the new concepts and experiences they meet and make against their own existing world pictures and, as they do so, adjust those constructs. One of the consequences of paying attention to the way learning works has been the recognition that the tangle of experiences of all kinds is the raw material from which we make the shaped thing we call knowledge, whether that is an everyday understanding of the world, or the more refined and abstracted patterns of thinking that make up the academic disciplines. The subjects of the school curriculum represent different ways of inspecting, organizing and extrapolating from the raw material: to accept them, learners need first to know that they have in their head a picture of the world that enables them to test, evaluate and make sense of the new ideas as they come. Otherwise they may not make anything at all of them.

We start from who and where we are now, inside our heads. As teachers we have to know where our students are; and we can best find that out by attending to what they say and write, as long as that talking and writing is allowed to follow the contours of thought and discovery. Some kinds of expression will inhibit learning and understanding if there is too much concentration on prescribed form and convention: other kinds will make it possible for inexperienced learners to make their own explorations. Here, for instance, thirteen-year-old Carl writes to his teacher about a passage read to the class from *The Teachings of Don Juan* by Carlos Castenada (Medway, 1980):

The thing that you read to us on Monday. I thought it was very interesting but somehow I don't think it could be true. Some parts could be true ... But if the things are true, why don't scientists go looking for them? And if it is all true it proves that the so-called red Indian isn't so primitive after all. Do you agree with me? And also there could be a lot to learn from them. And if all the other primitive peoples know things like this, it could open up a whole new science or range of studies. And I think that I might want to look into what the man's saying a little bit more. Although I think it can't be true, I have got a feeling it could be true. What do you think?

When we receive something as exploratory and complex as that, we rejoice. Reading it shows us something of what Carl understands about the world, and suggests a good deal about how to work with him. The chance to think aloud on paper to a sympathetic and responsive reader has given Carl the chance to make some new learning directions for himself – 'I think that I might want to look into what the man's saying a little bit more.'

We have not always perceived such writing as valuable. It was writers like Harold Rosen (Medway was one of his students) who showed us the force of evidence like this. Before that, teachers would have dismissed or even simply missed such writing, not seeing its power: they 'had the experience but missed the meaning'. Because they were not aware of what such evidence told them, they did not systematically create the conditions under which it might occur. Once they had seen the messages it carried they were more anxious to see more of it, and then change was inevitable.

Faced with this evidence, teachers had to become listeners and readers, not talkers or examiners. They had to pay attention to what their pupils were trying to do when they were talking or writing, to accept their present understandings and build on them, so that learners could reorganize the information they were presented with into comprehended knowledge. The approach affirms collaboration and negotiation, and the importance of *reconstructing knowledge* (Armstrong, 1977), as a process in which the students' grasp of particularity and the reality of their own direct experience is blended with the teacher's offering of generalizations and conceptualizations. As the two meet, the new is related to other particularities, and together they develop that pattern of particularities which is the learner's developing conceptual framework.

Today the importance of collaboration and negotiation needs to be reaffirmed because economic decline puts them in jeopardy. In a well-resourced and growing education system, society tolerates procedures which in times of anxiety it will question. During retrenchment, it seems, public, politicians and professionals tacitly agree that 'inessentials' can be discarded, but that what are identified as 'the basics' must be safeguarded, especially against teachers who are perceived by some politicians as standing for values opposed to those of economic individualism.

By 'the basics' is normally meant on the one hand a set of conventions concerning the appearance of writing – spelling, handwriting and punctuation – and on the other hand the ability to read, to count and perform arithmetical calculations, and to produce on demand clear, readable written language. These 'basics' are often perceived as 'tools': the feeling is that without them learning is impossible. Such a view is not supported by what we know about the way people learn. It *is* important, for social reasons if for no other, that children should be able to perform successfully in these ways, but not if they do so at the cost of more important abilities. Among these, as a very different set of 'basics', consider the ability to understand how learning operates; to be able to use various kinds of talk, appropriate to various public and private contexts; to grasp the importance of social context itself and its general influence upon language use; to write for different purposes and for different audiences, in various styles and forms; and to use complex reference systems. Even to define them like this still falls short of what it is we should covet for our children. What ought to be at the centre of attention is *what children's language can achieve for them*: things like the ability to use talk to get to know people they want to know, and to get on with those people they *have* to know; to use reading as a source of virtual experience, a way of living; to use both talking and writing as a means of discovering what they feel and think and of sharing that with others.

A policy that insists on narrowly observing social and linguistic conventions diminishes the chance of making these achievements available to children, obscures the quality of the education provided in schools, and can dismiss or trivialize the real achievements of teachers. It is because of the dangerous consequences of that policy that it seems even more necessary now to stress the importance of collaboration and negotiated learning, in which students and teachers work together to plan and define what is to be done.

Attention to 'the basics' should not entail didactic, authoritarian teaching based on unthinking repetitive routines. But the world at large associates the basics with 'good' dependable attitudes to education, to authority, and to society as a whole: and there can be apparently inexplicable tensions between professionals and the community at large, ostensibly centring on the question of 'standards' but probably caused by a deeper, ideological disagreement. A recent study of the problems faced by progressive schools, for instance (Fletcher *et al.*, 1985), suggests that when schools offered one model of learning and parents expected and wanted a different one, the parents felt that standards would decline and that their children would suffer from what the school was offering. Significantly, this anxiety is not confined to any one group of parents, though each group feels it has its own reasons for feeling dissatisfied: middle-class and working-class parents have both expressed anxiety publicly, as have Black parents. Maureen Stone, for example, speaks for those Black parents who felt that their children were being sold short by schools, and suggests that the establishment of Saturday schools was evidence of the dissatisfaction of Black parents with what state schools offered (Stone, 1980). This is one example of the tension between different views of 'standards'.

To define the matter as though the professionals understand and the general public does not over-simplifies the relationship between community and school and their respective contributions, and generates hostility between two groups which ought to be in partnership. In her seminal study *Ways with Words* Shirley Brice Heath indicates how easy it is for those who organize education systems, who 'look beyond [the immediate area] for rules and guidance' and are in touch with an international community of values, to put those values into operation without realizing how remote they may be from the people who will have to accept them during the course of schooling (Heath, 1983). The problem facing the teachers of the children in the two communities she describes is defined as being to 'understand their ways and to bring these ways into the classroom'. People who have a strong sense of local community-defined values but are not in touch with anything outside the community have no way of extending or testing their own values. The expansion and development that education should bring may seem more like an imposition of alien and irrelevant ideas. What is needed is for the teachers to be educated in the cultural models of the various groups they teach, and to see how to reconcile them with the overall purposes of education to 'change people's values, skills and knowledge bases' (Heath, ibid.) without cutting them off from their roots. This is never easy and may sometimes cause very different models of life and learning to come into conflict.

Certainly many communities have a straightforward definition of learning: it is about striving towards correctness and perfection. A ticked page of sums is better than a problem-solving approach to mathematics: a word-perfect reader is better than an imprecise one, whatever their respective understanding is; and rote-memorizing is better than intelligent guessing or prediction in reading. Successful learning is about having got it right. Those who see learning like that find it difficult to accept a very different model which welcomes and values risk-taking, inevitable and necessary error-making, and hypothesizing. To many people, this does not seem to be learning at all, but confusion, anarchy and a clear case of teachers casually abandoning children to the fate of being trapped by the limitations of their narrow view of the world.

It is hard for anyone who believes that learning is an incremental progression towards an externally defined perfection to accept the view being expressed in this book – that

all learning takes place through changes in the learner's existing model of the world

as Douglas Barnes puts it above; or, as James Britton says, that learners must bring with them

whatever [they] already know and believe and attempt to reinterpret that in the light of the evidence offered. Interpreting the new and reinterpreting the familiar are the two faces of one coin.

The sense of inevitable transience and change in these descriptions of learning make for very uncomfortable reading in those who prefer the world to be a fixed, permanent and predictable place. If individuals and cultural groups have a strongly shared model of learning and acculturation which affirms stability and the importance of accepting authority, they may react strongly against an educational system that tries to implement the model of learning presented in this book; and their reaction will be a nexus of personal emotion and socially shared cultural views.

Our schools, of course, contain children of many different cultural backgrounds, of different social classes and with different educational futures, both potential and actual. They always have, but that rarely seemed important when the task of education seemed to be to induct children happily into 'English' society, and when it was only the common professional culture of the teachers that mattered, not the culture of the learners. Each culture has brought with it both its own model of learning, and its own dialect of English or quite separate language: and it is to the issue of linguistic diversity, and how that relates to language and learning, that we turn now.

II

In the years since 1971 there have been many shifts of viewpoint due to our increased understanding of how gender, race and class affect and are affected by schools. In 1971 the major debate, generated largely by the work of Basil Bernstein, was whether working-class children were linguistically, and therefore educationally, disadvantaged. In one form or another, the argument has always been with us and perhaps always will be: there is a long tradition of ascribing children's failure to deficiencies in their language, and of ascribing such deficiencies to their working-class background. Bernstein's theory (Bernstein, 1971) was that there is a profound difference between 'elaborated' language and 'restricted' language, that the 'elaborated' language (or 'code', to use Bernstein's word) enables the user to handle complex ideas, and that there is a relationship between class and code: although we *all* guide our speech behaviour by means of a restricted code for much of the time, middle-class speakers use an elaborated code more naturally than working-class speakers. Thus the theory apparently reaffirmed the connection between class and educational failure.

The influence of the theory was great and the elegance of it was seductive.★ It is comforting, after all, to feel that an incurable problem inheres in the learners and that the school can do little to solve it.†

Notions of disadvantage grew powerfully alongside the ideological changes outlined above, and in the popular imagination they outpaced the alternative notions of valuing children's natural culture. Perhaps such reactions were, at least partly, unconscious responses to deep-felt anxieties in those teachers who were uncomfortable at accepting the moves towards openness that existed everywhere in the early 1970s; the notion of disadvantage at least declares the crucial significance of *teaching*. According to this theory, teachers can compensate for the disadvantage of their pupils.

Deficit theories have remained oppressive and still operate. Teachers try to do their best for every child in their class; but they will lower and limit expectations, and despair at ever changing the unchangeable, if they believe that the birthright of many of their children is severe cognitive deficiency, probably irreversible, because official reports and influential and important people tell them so. Failure becomes cast into the concrete foundations of the system.

Into the middle of this long debate about the role of language and social class in educational failure came children from families from Asia, the Caribbean, Africa, Mediterranean countries and elsewhere. There is a history still to be written about the ebb and flow of attempts to label and stereotype groups, or to reclaim for those same groups their essential dignity and opportunity. One after another, groups would be identified as being most 'in need' because most disadvantaged;

★ See Gordon's critique of verbal deficit theories (1981), which carefully charts their history and development and records their relationship with the debate about intelligence.

† There has been an interesting shift in educational theory in the years between 1970 and 1985. Then, prevailing theory, derived largely from Douglas (1964) and the Plowden Report (1966), stressed the dominating influence of the home and suggested that schools could do little to affect children. Child-rearing and social class were the controlling factors in a child's performance. Recent work such as Rutter's (1979) has suggested that schools *do* affect children's education, and has directed attention to the school's organization and general climate as factors in the educational success or failure of pupils.

once they were identified, support agencies would be established, finance would be made available; and, one by one, there was a tendency for those groups to prove themselves not at all disadvantaged but as competent as any other at surviving and succeeding. There was an international power struggle, as people relearned the old truth that power is vested in a dominant language, and that having access to that language, in the broadest sense, meant having access to power and self-determination. Otherwise, as Tony Harrison puts it in his poem 'National Trust' (Harrison, 1978),

> The dumb go down in history and disappear
> and not one gentleman's been brought to book:
>
> *Mes den hep tavas a-gollas y dyr*
> (Cornish) – 'the tongueless man gets his land took'

Harrison's use of the word 'man' to mean 'people' is a common usage. Yet it is an indicator of the problem faced by women in education in the way it ignores their existence. Women have been the largest disadvantaged group, cutting across race and class. They were never identified as disadvantaged, and never had support agencies established for them, despite indications from all the research that they were damaged by the educational system. More will be said about this later, but it is significant that the invisibility of the problem to policy makers affirms the rightness of Dale Spender's title *Invisible Women: The Schooling Scandal* (Spender, 1982). The whole issue of advantage and disadvantage became even more pointed because of the many-layered nature of the problem. Not only were working-class children or Black children likely to lose out in the system, but over half of each of those groups were girls, who were doubly at a disadvantage.★ If anyone was to be given attention, it was not likely to be them.

The presence of families of overseas origin extended the verbal deficit argument. No longer was it just a question of white working class: the language of minority ethnic groups could be included, too. If urban working-class children were verbally deprived, how much

★ Though this needs some qualification: Afro-Caribbean girls, for example, have perhaps not been as disadvantaged as Afro-Caribbean boys.

more deprived would be the children of Caribbean origin, bringing with them not only a non-standard form of English, but also a fundamentally different life-style from white children that was sure to put them at a disadvantage. As for Asian children, maintaining the language of the home would clearly be a threat and handicap to the all-important acquisition of standard English. There could even be the additional problem proposed for some children of being caught *between* languages, competent in neither, in a condition called 'semilingualism'. That some teachers persisted in accepting the culture and life-style their children brought with them to school, and in assuming as a matter of course that all of them were equally capable of learning, irrespective of their background, was an inevitable consequence of their commitment to the real lives of children. But it took a leap of the imagination to see positive advantages in the diversity and to build on it productively. Even for the committed teachers there were surprises as the full extent of the diversity became apparent.

When the first real surveys were undertaken, it was with real shock that the researchers saw the full range of languages represented: thirty-five different languages were commonly spoken among London school children (Rosen and Burgess, 1980), including Hakka, Ibo, Pushtu, Swahili and Tagalog, as well as the more predictable Urdu, Punjabi, Greek and Turkish. And these were only the most common languages: there were fifty-five altogether recorded in the London survey. This pattern was verified in all the surveys later undertaken by the Linguistic Minorities Project,★ and when the various dialects of English were included, the picture was indeed complex.

The diversity was even more complicated than it seemed. Consider a boy of sixteen who speaks Punjabi to his mother and grandmother, neither of whom speak English, but speaks English to his father and brothers at home, except when he shares with them in the ceremonies of their traditional culture on ritual occasions. At school he speaks English with a local accent in class, but when he is talking with his

---

★ The numbers of languages in the other surveys were as follows: sixty-four in Bradford, fifty in Coventry, eighty-seven in Haringey (with Greek and Turkish at the top of the list), forty-two in Peterborough, and sixty-five in Waltham Forest (Linguistic Minorities Project, 1983).

friends out of class they all share a version of the local Black dialect, a high-status language among their age-group. They never use that dialect where an adult can hear them. He is a fluent reader of English, and is also literate in Quranic Arabic. He is studying French at school and does quite well at it. If we ask what his dominant language is, or what his target language should be, what will he answer? And how is his school to recognize and reflect his life and linguistic competencies in its curriculum?

It is just as hard to ascribe cultures to children. Children will not always want to acknowledge their cultural origin: for every child proud to be Irish, or Sikh, or Jewish, or Greek Cypriot, or Rastafarian, there is another who prefers to be thought of solely as British. In some areas, all Black children will describe themselves as Jamaican, whatever Caribbean island they come from, because for them Jamaican culture has the highest status. For all these children, their language carries an additional charge, for it either affirms or denies a cultural identity. If the language, or dialect, or accent, is additionally seen as low status (Trudgill, 1976), the child may be reluctant to acknowledge it at all. Standard English has a status which depresses the value of other versions of English, although learning standard English does not make a child any more or less articulate or communicative. Even so, it is rare for Black dialects to be accorded the status George Fisher accords to them in his article (Fisher, 1983), where he quotes all his respondents in their own dialect. Those who are made dumb by attitudes to their language are in the same condition as those who live in a foreign country without speaking the language:

To many of these people, articulate as they were, the great loss was the loss of language – that they could not say what was in them to say. You have some subtle thought and it comes out like a piece of broken bottle. They could, of course, manage to communicate, but just to communicate was frustrating . . . 'I am left with myself unexpressed. My tongue hangs useless.' There was a terrible sense of useless tongue.

'The German Refugee', Bernard Malamud, *The Stories of Bernard Malamud*, Chatto, 1984.

The research, then, confirmed the informed observation of teachers:

despite the public status of English as the language of instruction there was a host of other languages. Many were spoken by large numbers of children, some only by one or two; but behind the languages lay a mixture of cultures and attitudes which inevitably affected the way children saw school and learning. It is not easy for a school to see what to do with information like this. What does it mean to teach physics or mathematics in a school where there are speakers of over thirty different languages? There are obvious implications for the curriculum in geography, in history, in English, in religious education: there could presumably be some reference to, or use of, the various cultural backgrounds of the children. But there is no agreement as to how this should be carried out and the debate has no easy resolution: it is not a question of finding a common language, because language and culture are indissolubly linked and there are contradictory views about the relationship between culture and curriculum.

What we must take as baseline assumptions are that there are speakers of languages other than English in our schools; that there are children who speak English as a first language but come from various ethnic backgrounds; and that the cultural assumptions of different cultural groups are often profoundly different but that on the whole they agree to accept schools as representing some kind of norm about learning and learning outcomes. Children will be affected by their school, but are never insulated from their culture and background: they derive their values from their community, and although they inevitably inspect and adjust those values as they meet new ideas and new ways of thinking and feeling through the education they receive, it must ultimately be the individual's decision as to whether he or she assimilates or rejects new values.

I said earlier that learners need to know that they have in their head a picture of the world. Active learning is, to repeat, an interaction between the student's own direct experience and the generalizations and conceptualizations offered by schooling. The culture and language of children's homes have major effects on their world pictures, and they will make different patterns and connections with new school experiences according to their different pre-existing patterns of experience. If they are to come to terms with what school offers, they need to perceive the significance of the cultural and linguistic diversity of all classrooms. The sensible place to begin any programme that aims to encourage effective learning must include some discussion with the students about the very existence of linguistic diversity; about what 'their own language' actually is and what it represents for them; and an acceptance of it as a resource rather than a handicap.* Thus, for example, removing bilingual learners from the classroom for small-group withdrawal work may be doubly damaging. It not only denies those children a full English-speaking context in which they could learn the language most successfully, it also removes the resource of diversity from the classroom, and reduces the curriculum possibilities that a multilingual classroom offers.

It is a central element in the theory of language across the curriculum that children must learn with their own language. The study of linguistic diversity shows the enormous range of dialects and versions of standard and non-standard English that exist, as well as the other languages. It is perhaps clear now that 'their own language' as an idea represents not just one thing, but several. It may be a child's mother tongue or dialect of English; it may be the way the child speaks at home as opposed to at school; it may be the voice of any child as opposed to the voice of the textbook. Effective learning could come to us in a very wide range of linguistic versions, all equally acceptable if we listen to their content not their form. Any attempt to construct a language policy which truly tries to reflect the linguistic diversity that exists in our schools must begin from a positive view of diversity. But that is only one strand in the complexity of what a language policy might be.

III

A language policy, unlike an insurance policy, is not a document full of paragraphs and sub-paragraphs, with indications of what is

---

* The Open University course, *Every Child's Language* (Open University Press), provides an in-service package to help teachers to do this.

permitted and forbidden, and instructions about how to deal with emergencies. It is like a political policy: a 'course of action adopted and pursued by a group; any course of action adopted as advantageous' (*OED*). It is a set of intentions constructed by the group who will abide by it, and it informs the behaviour of everyone who is party to the construction. It has never been possible to define in detail what a 'language policy' should be because, quite properly, policies vary from institution to institution depending on the intentions, interests, and problems of each one. They vary within outlines defined by general beliefs about language and learning and, like such beliefs, they may be implicit and inarticulate.

The theories outlined by Douglas Barnes and James Britton in the preceding papers have sometimes been introduced to schools. But a collection of theories about language does not itself represent a language policy. The policy is the set of intentions and proposed actions, and must come after a discussion of the general school policy and philosophy of education. A staff group must already be talking about education; the discussion of a language policy will then be a logical outcome of investigations of current practice.

First, teachers need to examine what is going on in their classrooms. When this is done, there is always a shock at discovering the differences between what is commonly thought to occur, and what is seen when experience is examined with a new conceptual framework. To learn that a student spends only about a minute a day on work-related talk, or that most of the texts provided for a group of twelve-year-olds are apparently too difficult for them (Lunzer and Gardner, 1979); or that 'an able [sixteen-year-old] had written 200,000 words in six subjects over four terms' (DES, 1979); or that girls consistently receive less attention in the classroom than boys, even if they have difficulties (Stanforth, 1981) – these are shocks. The discoveries about girls and what happens to them have been especially shocking. Stereotyped into areas of the curriculum deemed 'suitable', expected to behave in particular ways, treated in a manner that socializes them, consciously and unconsciously, into a style of being women that accords with a male-centred view of the world, and rendered invisible by an offical language of education that speaks constantly of pupil and teacher as 'he' – the 'man-made language' that Dale Spender identified (Spender, 1980) has been anatomized and seen to be of a piece with all the other attempts by one group to establish domination over another.

Pay attention to what really happens and, perhaps inevitably, one begins to examine one's own practice carefully and critically: it becomes apparent that pupils' problems in learning may be of the teachers' making, not caused by some deficiency in the learners. The patterns of communication in a lesson, and the roles that the teacher thereby ascribes to the student, are dominant factors in determining whether learning will or will not occur. The way the teacher speaks and, especially, asks questions; the kinds of task or written assignment set by the teacher; the kinds of textbook and worksheet presented; the opinions of their potential which teachers signal to girls, and the different attention that teachers give to different students; the working relationship between teacher and students and between the students themselves; the way the teacher organizes the furniture in the room and the distribution of time – these may all either support or impede the learner.

The major shift comes about when the teacher ceases to be concerned about the effectiveness of the teaching – in other words, when the teacher stops asking 'How do I look and seem to them?' and begins to ask 'What is happening to their learning?' Teaching is surrounded by fears: fear of making a fool of oneself, of losing control, of being hurt. The fear never wholly goes, but it becomes controllable and even productive when the focus of attention switches from self to students. Once the teacher has asked 'How can I help them to learn and understand?' then the answer is found by paying serious attention to what students are doing. And once one does begin to listen carefully and to read their written work responsively the fear begins to move away, because of the discovery that students do learn, but in ways that are unexpected and even unrecognized because they are not organized in the same way that teachers organize their teaching and are not as neat and tidy as expected.

With a certain inevitability, then, the paying of close attention to what students are saying and writing, and the close observation of *how* they read, write and talk, leads to the idea that pupils have things to say about their own processes of learning. If pupils are consulted about their views, they become partners in a process rather than passive receivers of information. Our job as teachers is to make the students' learning effective, so that the young people gradually and steadily acquire control over information, knowledge and events, and over themselves as learners, so they become people who know why they are doing what they do, and how to do it best. Teacher and learner together need to ask, what *kinds* of talk? of writing? of reading?

This process, or something like it, is what happens to the individual teacher; but the intention of language across the curriculum was always that it should be an institutional decision, not an individual one. And it is here that language across the curriculum never managed to become the widely held set of beliefs about teaching which many hoped would be the chief legacy of Chapter 12 of the Bullock Report, with its firm requirement in Recommendation 4 that

Each school should have an organized policy for language across the curriculum, establishing every teacher's involvement in language and reading development throughout the years of schooling.

Any new system of ideas and practice needs to be introduced into the existing system, and that means paying careful thought to the process of innovation and change. With hindsight, it appears now that the models of innovation implied by language across the curriculum carried their own failure with them. Failure is relative: many people were influenced by the ideas of language across the curriculum, it is true, and there are clear signs today in other developments that the long-term influences of those theories about the relationship between language and learning have been considerable.* But if the mark of success is widespread acceptance into the ordinary practice of the group, then language across the curriculum has not succeeded in becoming an orthodoxy. An analysis may help us to see both why

---

*See, for instance, as some examples of this, Active Tutorial Work; the Personal Development movement; the emphasis on negotiation and self-assessment in the new Certificates of Achievement; the increasing and officially approved use of course-work in examination courses; and the Cockcroft report (1982), with its emphasis on the place of talk in mathematical learning.

there was that comparative failure, and what might lead to a wider acceptance.

First, the ideas were often detached from the content of the curriculum and were offered as being exclusively about method. It seems obvious now that this would not appeal to subject teachers in secondary schools, who generally see themselves as having a body of content which they must, in some way, share with the students. Too often it was as though those who did not understand the problem of teaching from a clear body of content were urging those who did to take up an inappropriate teaching style for political rather than educational reasons. The suspicion this generated was encouraged by the tendency for it to look as though English teachers were trying to tell teachers of other subjects how to do their jobs.

Second, there was often a contradiction in the way the ideas were presented which mirrored the difficulty of establishing new models of learning. Douglas Barnes's continuum of teaching mentioned above describes the Transmission teacher and the Interpretation teacher. The Transmission teacher, Barnes suggests, feels that learning involved, the teacher in transmitting information to the learner who receives it: language acts as a vehicle for transmitting information to the recipient. The Interpretation teacher at the other end of the continuum sees the necessity for learners to reinterpret information into their own frame of reference by acting upon it, talking about it, writing about it, and making their own sense of it. It is clear from everything else in this book that language across the curriculum, if it was about anything, was about students making their own sense – 'interpreting'; and that it would be an important shift if teachers grasped the distinction and tried to act upon it.

Sometimes, though, the very people who believed in the 'interpretation' model and who were so opposed to the idea of teachers operating a transmission mode with their students, used that mode with a kind of righteous evangelical zeal to transmit the ideas of language across the curriculum to other teachers, and expected them to learn and be influenced by the ideas. But if learning operates in the ways the theories proposed, then teachers also needed to meet the theories in a way that encouraged learning. Teachers, too, must have the time to talk and share experiences, to consider these new ideas, draw their own conclusions and find ways of modifying their practice in the light of these conclusions.

Within an institution, organizational decisions have to be made if such discussion is to be possible. The decision-makers, responding to inexplicit pressures from society, have to be convinced that the topic is one worth discussion, so that it has a high enough priority to be given time. In the same way that there has never been a widespread policy conviction that the education of girls is a priority, so there has never been a national conviction about the importance of language across the curriculum. Despite the exhortation of the Bullock Report, that 'each school should have an organized policy for language across the curriculum . . .', there has never been the funding available for that to happen. Partly, this was because of the misunderstanding of what a 'policy' should be: many schools laid down an insurance policy, with written statements distributed to the whole staff, policy documents of one kind or another, together with a brief discussion of the *document*, rather than of the issues involved. It was then felt that the matter had been settled. The basic policy decision about what action should follow was never reached, and so teachers as a professional group did not form the new conceptualization that would have led them to see their pupils and their pupils' learning differently. To most of the people involved in those discussions – and there were a great many of them throughout the English-speaking world – it often seemed as if an interesting theoretical topic had been broached and then, because its relevance was not clear, abandoned.

There was probably another reason for the failure of language across the curriculum at an institutional level. It did, in fact, often look as though the ideas had been accepted, and as though the Transmission model was effective. But the effects were cosmetic. Although those who were proposing the ideas within a school generally understood the deeper structures, knew the complexities of the theories and saw the far-reaching implications, other staff too often saw only surface features, without having the opportunity to construct for themselves an understanding of the important underlying principles.

If complex ideas are innovated by people who have only an imperfect grasp of the deep structures, or of how to put them into practice, the result will always be imperfect. What are to the proposers of the innovation the inevitable problems of deep change, to be anticipated, planned for, and supported, become to the other group disturbing failures which lead them to reject both surface effects and deep structures. The surface features of the early parts of the process of introducing active learning seem to be disorganized, as students talk apparently aimlessly, write untidily and meander around topics instead of travelling in neat straight intellectual lines towards a final encapsulated topic. The uncertainty of the whole business is disturbing to those used to a far more controlled and teacher-directed procedure and, more important, it may also disturb the students themselves and their parents, because it looks so chaotic. Elizabeth Richardson gives a wise warning about this (Richardson, 1967):

> To what extent are the children aware of their own conflicting feelings of excitement and suspicion when they find themselves part of an experimental project? Do they welcome the uncertainties and the loss of known boundaries? Or do they suspect that their teachers are more concerned about the new methods than about the pupils on whom these methods are being tried? ... It is tempting to assume that the new methods are accepted by our pupils without question. But in fact the process of freeing pupils, whether children or adults, from the old familiar chains, is always painful as well as pleasurable. And when the experience is at its most puzzling, the adult in charge is likely to be blamed for incompetence or suspected of irresponsibility.

As Richardson makes clear, this warning applies to adults as well as children; and feelings like these can be threatening and disturbing for adults in positions of authority. The inevitable results of people learning are not received comfortably if they conflict, as they are bound to, with the way the institution normally organizes itself. It is significant, therefore, that one of the characteristics of recent political pressure in schools has been the various attempts to suppress controversy in general. The result is one of the oldest political and social tensions of all, neatly defined by Peter Medway (Medway, 1981):

> Its position [language across the curriculum's] is reminiscent of those earlier demands that the Bible be printed in English, not Latin, and that people be

allowed to discuss it and interpret it for themselves. We are responding as if our pupils had been saying, 'Talk to us in language we can understand, and give us the chance to use the resources and skills we already possess to make sense of the things you are showing and telling us.' . . . Denial of the opportunity to talk and write in personal modes is a reduction in the chance to learn. It is in effect a human rights issue.

A model of learning that *encourages* controversy, that has at its centre the essential requirement of thinking for yourself, and has deep structures which assert human rights, is always likely to come under assault.

Medway used the phrase 'personal modes' in his comment, and it is one that has led at times to misunderstanding. Personal modes are not, of course, full of personal pronouns, reference to the emotions and poetic adjectives. They are personal in the sense that thinking aloud is – a personal voice, observing the movement of thought and doing so in a language which captures the delicacy of discovery. Consider, for example, Nicola, a seventeen-year-old about to begin a history project on Charles I. Her writing is clearly thoughtful, based on wide understanding, and shows how she is prepared to follow her reflections without trying to make them into anything final. Had she, as Medway puts it, been denied the opportunity to write in this personal mode, she would have been denied the opportunity of making these discoveries (Levine, 1981).

On January 30th 1649 Charles I, King of England, Scotland and Wales, was executed.

Perhaps, in an age when the vague notion of the 'state' rested in the King, the personality of this particular monarch had been found lacking in the expression of government.

The motives for the execution were cloudy. Perhaps it was a comment on the king's own personality as expressed in his government.

Perhaps it was merely Parliament, and in a sense Cromwell, getting rid of a block to its power.

Perhaps it was the victory of the new order over the old. Perhaps this was the move which the writers of Magna Carta had foreseen and wished to avoid.

Perhaps it was legal murder.

Perhaps it was the result of a legal travesty.

Perhaps it was martyrdom.

Was it a revolution, or merely a rebellion?

Was it the final rejection of the institution of kingship?

Had it been a logical progression from the battlefield to the block?

Which side was fighting for whose liberty?

Could there have been another way out?

Was it the result of economic pressures?

Was it the result of religious pressures?

Was it to prevent further bloodshed?

How would it affect the constitution and the positions of kings and Parliaments?

Political expediency?

Moral necessity?

Was his fate decided before the trial?

This was the result of certain personalities as well as a game of high powered politics.

In terms of its effects today, was it the last strand of the divine right of kings, or was it the beginnings of democracy?

Who would you have supported?

Protecting the deep structures is therefore a task of some importance today, because otherwise everything founders. Douglas Barnes has reminded us above of what is at stake: the issues are

not of 'learning language' nor of 'extending vocabulary' but of giving or withholding access to the conceptual framework of a subject.

When a group of young people are vigorously involved in being fourteen years old in a science lesson, it is not always easy to see what sense they are making of the conceptual framework of a subject. We need some kind of explicit description of what the deep structures involve; or, to put that differently, what resources does a teacher need to be able to implement a language policy successfully?

First, the acceptance that a language policy that encourages the learning of students, as we have tried to outline in this book, is good for everybody: it is good for the highly successful academic who is bound for university, for bilingual learners, for disaffected and trucu-lent students, for slow learners.

Second, a language policy involves certain attitudes to what is being taught, and this depends to a large extent on the view that the teachers have of their own subject, and how engaged they are themselves in learning. People can be *practitioners* of a discipline – they may be art teachers who paint, history teachers who go on archaeological digs or spend time in the archives, science teachers who do research. Or they may be *students* – keeping up with the latest developments in their subject, reading contemporary literature, taking professional journals, joining professional associations. In either case, they will be committed intellectually and emotionally to what they are doing. Whatever else their students learn from them, they will learn what it means to take studying and learning seriously. But they may be neither practitioners nor students of their craft, and, to all intents and purposes, may have stopped learning: they merely teach what they themselves were taught, without asking why. The effects of this on the students' learning can be grave:

> He who learns from one occupied in learning, drinks from a running stream. He who learns from one who has learned all he is to teach, drinks the green mantle of the standing pool.
>
> A. J. Scott (1805–66)*

If students are to discover what learning is, they need to be in touch with someone for whom the possibility of learning is a felt reality.

Finally, successful teachers will have considered the nature of learning. It is not that they know exactly where the students will be at the end of the journey, but they know how to start their students on the exploration. They recognize and tolerate the individual directions that each learner must take, and know how much support the learner needs. One form that the support can take is to recognize the importance of process as opposed to product, because it is the process that has most effect on the learner.

Although the products of learning – the essay, the new concept remembered and rehearsed, the test successfully achieved – are important to the teacher, what is important to learners, if they are allowed to

*A. J. Scott was principal of Owen College, Manchester, and co-founder of the Manchester Working Men's College.

perceive their value by teachers who do not insist that education should be product-centred, is the process of learning. The talk students have with each other, and with the teacher as someone who knows more than they do; the writing in which they tell themselves things at the same time as they tell their reader; the group discussions and arguments in which students test out their new understandings – these are more important to the learner than the well-formed elegant essay which satisfies the teacher or the examiner. In the course of such processes, any learner is bound to be uncertain and tentative; but classrooms should be places that can support uncertainty.

IV

Whatever the relationships between education and society, schools are models – microcosms – of the world they inhabit. They can also be models of worlds that *might* be inhabited. The prevailing ideologies of a culture are always reflected in some way within a school, but the secure world of the school can represent alternative styles of being to its children. So a discussion of putting some of the ideas in this book into practice is also a discussion about an implied society. Schools *are* worlds for children for eleven years of their life.

What then would a school look like which has tried to put those ideas into practice? What would you see if you could peer into the classrooms? What would you hear if you eavesdropped on children and teachers talking together? If you read responsively what the children wrote, what would you read? What would parents and the general community feel about it all?

First, you would see people talking to each other a good deal. Groups of children would be working together, in and out of classrooms: sometimes they would be talking to each other, sometimes to the teacher or another adult, who might be a parent or a visitor brought in especially for the children to welcome, to question, to see as a resource. Teachers would be sitting with a group, or talking to an individual. The topics of the conversation would range from complex analysis of new ideas, through discussion of current work, to very personal subjects.

Discussions about personal feelings and viewpoints are the most absorbing, the most necessary, but sometimes the most threatening of all. A curriculum which does not as a matter of course provide students with the opportunity to rehearse, revalue and reorganize their thoughts and feelings disables them, cutting them off from the most important process of all. This is so whether what is under discussion is complex and abstract ideas or personal experiences. Listen, for example, to Fatima and Maria, two girls of seventeen, talking to Jane Miller (Miller, 1983). They are talking about the relationship between language and context, and about which language (they are bilingual) they use on different occasions; but they are also examining their own lives:

JM   Supposing I were to suggest your doing an imitation of you talking to your Dad. What language would you do it in?
Fatima I'd want to do it in English because, as I've said, I don't feel in English in a dangerous state, but then I wouldn't dare to say it in English, so I'd just forget about it.
Maria You just have to clam up and hold on.
JM   Do you think this is a cultural thing or do you think it's you and your Dad or d'you think it's men and women, or what?
Maria For me I think it's me and my Dad.
Fatima For me it's men and women and lots of it, I'm talking personally, is Dad and daughter. The way they look at women. You're a girl, shut up, you go and see what your Mum's doing.

That interaction between intellect and feeling is crucial to learning, and something similar needs to happen in all areas of the curriculum. In mathematics and science, there may be very personal kinds of writing and talking going on as children make sense of their learning; because the topics are more abstract, the personal quality of the response will lie in the form and language, not in expressions of emotion. Feelings still come through, even so. Here, for instance, two eleven-year-old boys have investigated the relationship between cubes and their area, and drawn a graph of their findings. They wrote about it triumphantly, like this:

We did a graph about HOW CUBES GROW and this is what we found out about the graph and HOW CUBES GROW.

We found out that the result is a curved line. If you could imagine the curve getting longer, what would happen? It would become steeper and if it got even larger it would get even more steeper. So we've found out one thing, the larger it gets the steeper it goes.

What do you think it's trying to do? Will it ever do what it's trying to do? It is trying to reach a vertical axis because the larger it gets the steeper it becomes. Now you know more about HOW CUBES GROW.

And here is a group of thirteen-year-old girls in a home economics lesson (Robertson, 1980), revising what they know about water and discussing their working concepts of surface tension and detergent. Notice how they shift between abstract statements and personal anecdote, how they construct collaboratively what no one of them could have done alone, and how much they trust their own voices:

PUPIL 1   What do we know about water?
VOICE   Don't know.
PUPIL 1   Water's got surface tension.
VOICE   Yes.
VOICE   And you can get hard and soft.
PUPIL 1   Water won't soak into garments without –
VOICES   [*interrupting*] – a detergent.
VOICE   It will.
PUPIL 2   It won't, not properly, because the detergent breaks the surface tension.
PUPIL 1   If you notice when you wash your hair – this is a good example because I found this – when you wash your hair water doesn't soak through your hair, you've still got bits that's still dry, haven't you, but as soon as you put one lot of shampoo on your hair will just go automatically wet.
VOICES   Yes, won't it?
VOICES   Yes.
PUPIL 1   That's what I always find, anyway.
PUPIL 2   That's the same as with materials though, isn't it, because as soon as you put the detergent in the water the surface tension breaks and then the material gets wet, properly wet I mean.

A good many of the discussions are likely to be about learning itself.

There will be a constant reflection on what has been going on, an interrogation of both the process and the product of teaching and learning. Teachers who have grasped the significant connections between thought, language and learning, and seen the importance of 'debriefing', of standing back from their learning and inspecting it, will make sure opportunities for that are constantly provided. Anne Baker, a teacher of eight- to nine-year-olds, gives Dawn that opportunity in their regular session together as 'Dawn reads to her teacher' (Baker, 1984):

T. Um. *Charlotte's Web*. Are you still thinking about it?
[*Dawn considers a book she's had difficulty coming to terms with* (This doesn't happen every time.)]
D. Yes.
T. Go on.
[*an open prompt to let Dawn specify her own area of concern*]
D. Thinking about when she died.
T. Tell me about it.
D. Well Wilbur was calling her and I think she fell off the wooden ledge bit and Wilbur started crying. I started crying then.
T. Just then.
D. Yes. Have you got a favourite bit in *Charlotte's Web*?
[*now Dawn takes the initiative to make the conversation a genuinely shared experience*]
T. Who me? Mm. I think the bit I like the best is when Charlotte meets Wilbur for the very first time and he hasn't seen her and . . .
D. 'Wait until morning. You'll see me.'
T. That's right. 'Wait until morning and you'll see me.' And he wakes and he's very impatient when he wakes and then she says, 'Salutations.' And he doesn't know what it means. 'Salut what?' he says. And then he does really meet her. I think that's my favourite bit.
D. Mm. And she dies and when all her children hatch he says, 'Salutations,' to them.
T. Yes he does, doesn't he.

There are, then, complex kinds of formal and less formal talk going on, as well as the informal talk that pervades any institution. In general, the talk is serving many different functions: sometimes – as for Dawn and her teacher, or Fatima and Maria with Jane Miller – it is intrinsically satisfying as a way of sorting out thoughts and feelings. Sometimes, as for the girls doing home economics, it is a way of solving a problem, of sharing and negotiating ideas. On other occasions, it will be a sensitizing process before writing, or a way of exploring an experience and conceptualizing it.

Writing, too, will serve a whole complex of functions in our ideal but mythical school. Sometimes, as for Anil and Steven writing about their cubes graph, it is a kind of triumphant celebration of learning. In some lessons, we will see children being asked to jot down their earliest responses to a new experience and then compare their notes with each other; sometimes, they will be writing logbooks, thinking aloud, so to speak, about their learning as they go, supported by a responsive and insightful teacher:

6/2 Friday

Today there were no geography lessons so I stayed in humanities so I carried on with those questions which you gave us on Wednesday. Thank you for explaining the questions to us.

Anyway I have now finished those questions so I have handed it in to be marked.

9/2 Monday

I am really getting to like this project. I really like those typed sheets you give us. I have really learnt a lot since I have been doing these sheets, they are great.

I am pleased I decided to do this project.

Yes I get the impression you've learnt a lot, too. So have I, reading the stuff in order to write the sheets, and then having to explain them. I find sociology an exciting subject to read at the moment.

The next sheets are now ready!

18/2 Wednesday

Today I have been doing geography all morning. So I will see you on Monday so you can explain the second work sheet on Juvenile Delinquency.

20/2 Friday

This morning I started to answer the questions on the Juvenile Delinquency – second sheet but I would like you to explain this to me. (Later.) Now you have explained to me I can understand the sheet. Thank you. I am taking the sheet home to finish off because I want to do that longer assignment at home so I can spend more time on it and I can think about it more.

Thus Julie, aged fifteen, writing to her teacher Peter Medway (Medway, 1980). It is a style of writing in which students can not only explore ideas but can also practise the whole business of writing itself; by having a real reader, one acquires the sense of the 'internalized other' (Mead, 1934) that enables the writer to predict and cope with the anticipated reader's response, and so to be successful.

Learners will not be expected to deal with new ideas immediately in fully-formed and shaped essays, but will have the opportunity to move towards it in the ways that we have come to see are necessary in all writing: an early thinking-aloud form, the chance to talk to others about it, the chance to try out different forms and styles. They will be writing for the teacher but also for each other, and sometimes for audiences outside the school.

The parents of the students will know what's going on. The school will be explaining to them what the meaning is of classroom activities, and why the teachers do what they do: the lessons of Tizard and Hughes (Tizard and Hughes, 1984) and Brice Heath (Heath, 1984) – that parents not only have something to say about their children's education, but something to tell teachers about how it might be done – will have been learnt. And the same process of collaborative involvement will be shared by the teachers, too, as the triangle of child, parent and teacher works together on the education of the child.

Accountability of the best kind will be taken for granted: teachers will be prepared to explain what they do and why they do it, without expecting to fulfil imposed demands. That teachers must learn, and need time to do so, cannot be stressed too much; nor can the importance of teachers sharing what they are learning with each other and their students. There should be a counterpoint of equal and non-competitive interests, all combining to create the whole.

Throughout the three papers of this book, we have stressed the way the learner constructs a world. That personal construct is constantly interacting with the perceived real world and adjusting itself to it; the picture of the world that children receive has a major effect on the internal version of it they are constantly constructing. If the world repeats constantly, in measured tones, that girls are inferior to boys, that Black is inferior to White, then that is the message that is added to the picture. If the messages about learning stress the necessity of passive acceptance and devalue the everyday knowledge the student already possesses, then the students will feel that only what their teachers know is of importance and that what they know themselves is insignificant.

It will be clear by now that we believe there is a social importance to the style of teaching and learning we are proposing. It is not, let us say clearly, a new message: as James Britton pointed out (Britton, 1978), it is not

part of any bandwagon, or fashion cycle, or pendulum swing; it is a slowly growing movement with philosophical roots way back in the past.

But the lengthy tradition does not prevent it from coming under attack. The ideological differences between proposed systems are sensed even if they are not explicitly grasped, and as Polanyi indicated (Polanyi, 1973):

A hostile audience may deliberately refuse to entertain novel conceptions because its members fear that once they have accepted this framework they will be led to conclusions which they rightly or wrongly abhor.

But it was also Polanyi who defined the way forward, in a statement that may well stand as an epigraph for this book:

Proponents of a new system can convince their audience only by first winning their intellectual sympathy for a doctrine they have not yet grasped. Those who listen sympathetically will discover for themselves what they would otherwise never have understood.

'Discovering for themselves' is what all learners have to do. It is what readers of this book must do if they are to test for themselves the truths of what we have been saying.

Acknowledgements

My thanks to those friends who have advised and helped me in the writing of this: Donald Fry, Hilary Minns, Andrew Stibbs, and of course Douglas Barnes and Jimmy Britton themselves.

Bibliography

Armstrong, M. (1977), 'Reconstructing Knowledge' in *The Countesthorpe Experience*, ed. Watts, J., Unwin Education.

Baker, A. (1984), 'Dawn reads to her teacher' in *Children Reading to their Teachers*, National Association for the Teaching of English.

Baldwin, J., and Wells, H. (1979), *Active Tutorial Work*, Basil Blackwell, for Lancashire County Council.

Bernstein, B. (1971), *Class, Codes and Control*, Routledge & Kegan Paul.

Britton, J. (1978), 'Foreword' in *Teaching for Literacy: Reflections on the Bullock Report*, ed. Davis, F., and Parker, R., Ward Lock Educational.

Department of Education and Science (1967), *Children and their Primary Schools (The Plowden Report)*, HMSO.

Department of Education and Science (1975), *A Language for Life (The Bullock Report)*, HMSO.

Department of Education and Science (1979), *Aspects of Secondary Education in England. A Survey by HM Inspectors of Schools*, HMSO.

Department of Education and Science (1982), *Mathematics Counts (The Cockcroft Report)*, HMSO.

Douglas, J. W. B. (1964), *The Home and the School*, MacGibbon and Kee.

Fisher, G. (1983), 'Language in political context: the case of West Indians in Britain' in *Oxford Review of Education*, vol. 9. no. 2.

Fletcher, C., Caron, M., and Williams, W. (1985), *Schools on Trial: the trials of Democratic Comprehensives*, Open University Press.

Gordon, J. C. B. (1981), *Verbal Deficit: A Critique*, Croom Helm.

Harrison, T. (1978), 'National Trust' in *The School of Eloquence*, Rex Collings.

Heath, S. B. (1983), *Ways with Words*, Cambridge University Press.

Kelly, G. (1963), *A Theory of Personality*, Norton, New York.

Langer, S. (1942), *Philosophy in a New Key*, Harvard University Press.

Linguistic Minorities Project (1983), *The Schools Languag Survey: Summary of Findings From Five LEA's Tinga Tinga Books*, Heinemann Education.

Levine, N. (1981), *Language, Teaching and Learning: History*, Ward Lock Educational.

Lunzer, E., and Gardner, K. (1979), *The Effective Use of Reading*, Heinemann Education.

McLuhan, M. (1974), *Understanding Media*, Abacus Books.

Malamud, B. (1984), 'The German Refugee' in *The Stories of Bernard Malamud*, Chatto and Windus.

Mead, George H. (1934), *Mind, Self and Society*, University of Chicago Press.

Medway, P. (1981), 'The Bible and the Vernacular', *English in Education*, vol. 15, no. 1.

Medway, P. (1980), *Finding a Language. Autonomy and Learning in School*, Chameleon Books, Writers and Readers.

Miller, J. (1983), *Many Voices. Bilingualism, Culture and Education*, Routledge & Kegan Paul.

Open University (1985), *Every Child's Language*, Open University Press.

Polanyi, M. (1969), *Personal Knowledge. Towards a Post-Critical Philosophy*, Routledge & Kegan Paul.

Richardson, E. (1967), *Group Study for Teachers*, Routledge & Kegan Paul.

Robertson, I. (1980), *Language Across the Curriculum: Four Case Studies*, Schools Council Working Paper 67, Methuen Educational.

Rosen, H. (1971), *Language, the Learner and the School*, Penguin.

Rosen, H., and Burgess, T. (1980), *Languages and Dialects of London School Children*, Ward Lock Educational.

Rutter, M., Maugham, B., Mortimore, P., Ouston, J., and Smith, A. (1979), *Fifteen Thousand Hours*, Open Books.

Spender, D. (1980), *Man Made Language*, Routledge & Kegan Paul.

Spender, D. (1982), *Invisible Women: The Schooling Scandal*, Writers and Readers.

Stanworth, M. (1981), *Gender and Schooling: A Study of Sexual Divisions in the Classroom*, Explorations in Feminism no. 7, Women's Research and Resources Centre.

Stone, M. (1980), *Teaching the Black Child in Britain*, Fontana.

Tizard, B., and Hughes, M. (1984), *Young Children Learning: Talking and Thinking at Home and at School*, Fontana.

Trudgill, P. (1975), *Accent, Dialect and the School*, Arnold.

Vygotsky, L. (1962), *Thought and Language*, MIT Press.

DATE DUE

HIGHSMITH   #LO-45227